EXCEL 2024

From Beginner to Pro A Step-by-Step Guide Through Formulas and Functions with Real-World Applications and Expert Advice

Daniel Parker

TABLE OF CONTENTS

PREFACE

ACKNOWLEDGMENTS

In the serene early morning hours, long before the buzz of daily obligations takes hold, I often find myself reflecting on the journey that led to the creation of this book. "Excel 2024: From Beginner to Pro" is not just a compilation of knowledge about Microsoft Excel; it's a tapestry woven from many threads, contributed by a host of remarkable individuals whose expertise and encouragement have been indispensable.

Firstly, I must express my gratitude to my family. Their unyielding support and understanding have been my anchor through countless late nights and early mornings spent crafting the pages you hold today. My wife, Ellen, has been especially instrumental, providing both critique and encouragement, ensuring that each chapter serves its purpose and resonates with clarity and usefulness.

The genesis of this book was, in many ways, sparked by my colleagues and mentors in the field of data analytics. I owe a particular debt to Dr. Emily Stanton, a pioneer in predictive analytics, whose groundbreaking work inspired the section on data modeling. Her insights into leveraging Excel for predictive analysis transformed my approach and, I hope, will elucidate new pathways for you, the reader, in your professional endeavors.

I am also profoundly grateful to my professional network, especially the members of the Advanced Data Analysis forum. Their relentless curiosity and peer reviews have not only sharpened the content of this guide but also broadened my own understanding of Excel's evolving capabilities. It is through lively debates and shared experiences with peers like Michael Zheng and Lisa Monroe that the chapters on advanced formulas and macros were born.

A significant portion of the practical applications cited in this book are drawn from real-world challenges faced by industry experts. I thank each one of them for allowing me to include their case studies and for their invaluable feedback, which has greatly enhanced the book's applicability in everyday business scenarios. Notable among them is Jonathan Hill, whose expertise in financial modeling has enriched the sections dealing with complex financial forecasts and budgeting techniques.

The development of this book was also made possible by the skilled professionals at Pearson Publishing. My editor, Sarah Golding, deserves special mention for her keen eye and editorial wisdom. Her guidance was critical in structuring the book in a way that best serves both novice users and seasoned analysts.

The design team, led by Mark O'Neill, transformed my vision for a clear, accessible guide into a beautifully formatted reality that you, as a reader, can navigate with ease.

In preparing this manuscript, I relied heavily on the latest software tools and resources that have been developed to keep pace with Excel's advancements. I extend my gratitude to the developers and IT professionals who work behind the scenes to make these tools available and effective. Their innovations make the sophisticated techniques discussed in this book possible and practical.

I must also acknowledge the global Excel community. Through countless forums, workshops, and conferences, your enthusiasm and insights have continuously pushed the boundaries of what can be achieved with this powerful tool. Your stories of success and struggle alike have been integral in shaping the narrative and strategies laid out in this book.

In addition to the professional and personal support, I would be remiss if I didn't mention the academic and training institutions that foster the next generation of Excel experts. These institutions are the breeding grounds for innovative ideas and applications in data analytics. Their research and training materials have been a great resource, often providing a foundation for the tutorials and examples used throughout this book.

Lastly, I want to thank you, the reader. Your commitment to enhancing your skills and your trust in this book to guide you through the complex landscape of Excel 2024 is deeply appreciated. Whether you are just beginning your journey or are looking to refine advanced skills, it is for you that this book was written. Your feedback, success stories, and even critiques are what motivate me to continue exploring, learning, and sharing knowledge in the ever-evolving field of data analytics.

As we turn the page together on this new edition, it is my hope that the skills and insights you gain will not only advance your career but also inspire you to contribute to the collective knowledge of our community. Just as I have stood on the shoulders of giants to craft this guide, may it serve as a stepping stone for your own achievements and explorations in data analysis. Thank you for being a part of this journey.

HOW TO USE THIS GUIDE

Embarking on a journey through Excel 2024 is akin to setting out on a grand exploration of a vast and vibrant city. Each chapter in this guide acts as your map, highlighting diverse districts—from the foundational setups of simple spreadsheets to the intricate skyscrapers of advanced data analysis. As you traverse through this book, you'll encounter paths that can transform the novice into a savvy user and the experienced analyst into an expert.

To harness the full potential of this guide, approach it as you would a practical workshop. The book is structured to progressively build your skills, layering complexity as you move forward, yet it's also crafted to allow for targeted learning. Whether you are in urgent need to resolve a specific problem or wish to methodically enhance your proficiency, this guide adapts to your needs.

Imagine you're learning to drive. Initially, mastering the vehicle and understanding the rules of the road are paramount. Similarly, the initial sections of this book focus on the essentials of Excel 2024. You'll start by familiarizing yourself with the updated interface and basic functions. Just as a driver doesn't need to know how to rebuild an engine to navigate the streets, you won't need to dive into complex macros or advanced formulas right away.

As you gain confidence, the chapters will introduce more sophisticated tools and techniques. This is comparable to learning to navigate through traffic or drive in challenging conditions. The sections on data analysis, for example, will equip you with the skills to not only understand but also to manipulate and present data in ways that can significantly impact your professional reports and decisions.

For those who thrive on detailed exploration, chapters dedicated to advanced Excel functions, such as Power Pivot and macro scripting, will be akin to off-road driving—challenging yet thrilling. These sections are designed to elevate your skills beyond conventional use, enabling you to automate tasks, manage larger datasets, and create more complex models.

Each chapter is designed to be self-contained, allowing you to either progress through the book in sequence or to focus on particular areas that are immediately relevant to your work or interests. At the beginning of each chapter, you'll find a brief overview of what to expect and how it builds upon previous chapters or prepares you for subsequent topics. This way, you can easily decide how deep to dive based on your current needs or time constraints.

To facilitate learning, each topic is supplemented with step-by-step instructions, real-world examples, and tips on troubleshooting common issues. These practical elements are not just add-ons; they are integral parts of the learning process, ensuring that you can apply what you learn directly to real-world tasks. For instance, when discussing formulas, the book will not only show how to create them but also how to deploy them effectively across different scenarios like financial forecasting or inventory management.

The end of each chapter features exercises designed to reinforce the concepts introduced. These are not mere academic drills; rather, they reflect typical problems you might encounter in the workplace. Completing these exercises will not only solidify your understanding but also enhance your problem-solving skills, making you more adept at using Excel as a powerful tool in your professional arsenal.

Moreover, the guide is peppered with insights from industry experts, anecdotes from my own experiences, and feedback from users like you. These stories do more than just embellish; they provide context, illustrate common pitfalls, and offer inspiration. They show how Excel skills can directly enhance job performance, support career advancement, and facilitate a more efficient handling of data.

In the spirit of continuous improvement—a core principle in both data analysis and professional development—the final sections of this guide invite you to challenge your newfound skills through a series of progressively complex projects. These challenges are designed to be approached after you have navigated through the earlier chapters, acting as a capstone to your learning experience. Finally, as you make your way through "Excel 2024: From Beginner to Pro," remember that the ultimate goal of this guide is not just to impart knowledge, but to empower you to use that knowledge effectively. By the end of this book, Excel should feel less like a software program and more like a versatile tool that's essential to your analytical toolkit—one that you can wield with confidence and creativity in your pursuit of data-driven solutions.

EXCEL 2024: WHAT'S NEW?

As we stand at the precipice of yet another year, Excel remains not just relevant but essential, evolving continuously to meet the demands of modern data analysis and business needs. The release of Excel 2024 brings with it an array of new features and enhancements that promise to redefine how professionals like you navigate data, implement analysis, and present results. These updates are not just incremental improvements but are pivotal changes that cater to the evolving landscape of technology and workplace demands.

One might wonder, why does Excel need to update so frequently? The answer lies in the very nature of our work environments that are increasingly data-driven and require more robust, intuitive tools. Microsoft's commitment to this demand is evident in Excel 2024, which introduces features designed to streamline workflows, enhance analysis, and improve collaboration across platforms.

A significant update in this version is the enhancement of the co-authoring capabilities. Remember the times when sharing an Excel file meant risking overwrites or losing track of who added what? Those days are becoming a distant memory. Excel 2024's advanced co-authoring features allow multiple users to work on the same file simultaneously, with real-time updates and communication. This feature isn't just about tracking changes; it's about integrating teamwork seamlessly into the fabric of the software.

The practical implications are profound, especially for projects requiring collaborative input from various stakeholders, such as budgeting exercises or cross-departmental reporting.

Another exciting development is the introduction of advanced data types. Excel 2024 goes beyond text, numbers, and formulas to include types like 'Geography' and 'Stocks.' These aren't merely data labels; they're smart, context-aware types that understand and assimilate relevant external data into your spreadsheets. Imagine inserting a company's stock ticker symbol and seeing Excel pull in its current stock price, financials, and latest news without needing to leave your spreadsheet. This feature not only saves time but also integrates a richer, more dynamic layer of information.

Artificial Intelligence (AI) has also made its way more deeply into Excel with the new and improved Excel Assistant. Building on the foundations laid by previous versions, this AI tool can now understand and execute more complex queries. You can ask, "What was the percentage increase in sales from last month?" and the Assistant not only computes it but also suggests creating a trend analysis graph. This integration of AI helps in transforming raw data into actionable insights more efficiently, making advanced analytics accessible to users without extensive technical expertise.

The customization capabilities have also seen a significant upgrade. Excel 2024 introduces a more intuitive approach to UI customization, allowing users to tailor the workspace to their specific needs. This means not only rearranging and adding tools to the ribbon but also creating fully personalized tabs that can include your most-used functions and macros. This kind of customization is akin to setting up your workstation: it aligns with your workflow preferences and makes you more efficient.

For those of you intrigued by the potential of data visualization, Excel 2024 introduces new chart types and styles, including dynamic arrays and enhanced conditional formatting options that make interpreting data at a glance easier and more intuitive. These tools are not just about making prettier charts; they are about making the visualization of complex datasets easier to understand and manipulate.

The formula engine in Excel 2024 has been re-engineered to enhance its calculation speed and incorporate a smarter formula suggestion feature. As you type, Excel not only predicts the formula but also provides a quick preview of the result, an invaluable feature when dealing with large datasets where each calculation can be time-consuming.

For those deep into data manipulation, the Power Query feature has been made more robust, supporting a wider array of data sources and offering more sophisticated data shaping capabilities.

This enhancement is crucial for professionals dealing with diverse data types and sources, ensuring that Excel can act as a comprehensive tool for data consolidation and transformation.

Lastly, Excel's integration with other Microsoft tools like Power BI has been tightened. Excel 2024 allows for smoother data export to Power BI, enabling more complex data modeling and reporting capabilities. This synergy is particularly valuable for those looking to leverage Excel for preliminary data analysis before scaling their findings across the broader organizational context using Power BI.

These features and updates in Excel 2024 underscore a pivotal shift in how data is handled and presented, emphasizing collaboration, efficiency, and powerful data processing capabilities. As you navigate through the chapters of this guide, keep these enhancements in mind. They are not merely tools, but bridges to greater productivity and deeper insights, designed to empower you, the user, to excel in every aspect of your data-driven endeavors. With each page, you'll discover not just how to use these features, but how to make them a seamless extension of your analytical skillset.

PART I: GETTING STARTED WITH EXCEL 2024

1. INTRODUCTION TO EXCEL 2024

UNDERSTANDING THE INTERFACE

When first opening Excel 2024, the sleek and modern interface might feel slightly intimidating. Yet, this initial complexity belies an intuitive layout designed to enhance user efficiency and accessibility. As we delve into the interface of Excel 2024, imagine yourself as a pilot in the cockpit of a sophisticated aircraft; while there are many controls, each serves a specific purpose to ensure a smooth flight. Understanding how to navigate this interface is the first step in mastering Excel to make your data analysis both efficient and effective.

At the heart of Excel's interface is the Ribbon, a dynamic tool panel that houses all the features necessary for spreadsheet manipulation. The Ribbon organizes tools into logical groups, each housed in tabs such as 'Home', 'Insert', 'Data', and 'Review'. Each tab is tailored to facilitate specific types of tasks, which helps in reducing clutter and focusing on the task at hand. For instance, the 'Home' tab provides quick access to commonly used functions like formatting, copying, and pasting, while the 'Data' tab focuses on tools related to data management including sorting, filtering, and importing.

The adaptability of the Ribbon in Excel 2024 is noteworthy. It can be customized to better fit your workflow, allowing you to create personal tabs with your most frequently used commands. This customization not only streamlines your workflow but also makes the tools you need more accessible, significantly enhancing productivity.

Below the Ribbon lies the Formula Bar, a critical component when working with Excel. This area displays the data or formula contained in the active cell, and it's where you can edit them directly. The Formula Bar also provides features like formula auditing and cell locking, crucial for maintaining the integrity of your data manipulations.

The main area, or the 'spreadsheet grid', is where data lives and breathes. Here, columns and rows intersect to form cells, each capable of storing data points, formulas, and even images. The seemingly endless grid is intuitively designed, with each cell identifiable by a unique address based on its row number and column letter, a setup that simplifies data referencing in formulas and functions.

Another subtle yet powerful aspect of the Excel 2024 interface is the Name Box located to the left of the Formula Bar. This small box is more significant than it appears, allowing you to navigate quickly to different cells or ranges by typing in references directly. Additionally, you can name ranges of cells for easier use in formulas, a feature that becomes invaluable as your data sets grow larger and more complex.

The status bar at the bottom of the Excel window is another tool that is easy to overlook but packed with functionalities. It offers immediate insights into selected data, such as sum, average, and count, without needing to insert formulas manually. It can also be customized to show only the information relevant to your current task, keeping you informed about the status of your data at a glance.

For those who manage large datasets, the View tab provides tools that are essential for maintaining an overview of your work. Features like 'Freeze Panes' allow you to keep an area of your spreadsheet visible while you scroll through the rest of your document, which is invaluable when working with extensive data where headers need to remain visible.

The introduction of the 'Tell Me' feature, represented by a light bulb icon, is another innovation in Excel 2024 that streamlines workflow. This tool acts like a personal assistant within Excel, where you can type what you want to do (e.g., "filter data", "apply conditional formatting") and it provides you with the options or commands to execute the task directly. It's particularly useful for new users or those who may not remember where specific tools are located within the Ribbon.

Lastly, Excel 2024 has enhanced its support for accessibility, ensuring that users with disabilities can also navigate and use Excel efficiently. The 'Accessibility Checker' on the Review tab helps identify and fix any parts of your spreadsheet that might not be easily readable or navigable by people with disabilities, which not only helps in making your work more inclusive but also more professional.

By understanding each of these components and their purposes, you can begin to feel more at home with Excel 2024's interface. Just like a pilot becoming familiar with the controls of their aircraft, getting to know the interface of Excel is the first step in your journey toward mastering this powerful tool. From here, each feature and function builds upon this foundational knowledge, enabling you to handle your data tasks with precision and efficiency.

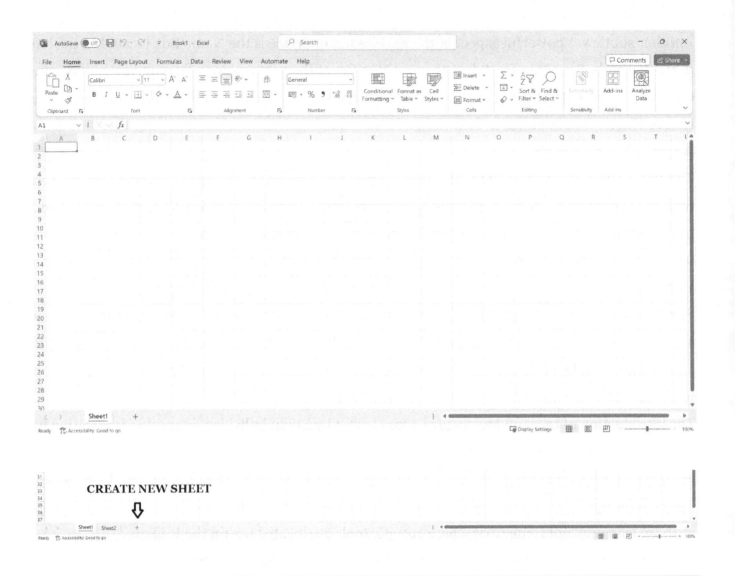

CREATE NEW SHEET

ESSENTIAL EXCEL TERMINOLOGY

Diving into the world of Excel 2024, it's akin to learning a new language—one where each term and concept opens up countless possibilities for analyzing and managing data efficiently. To truly harness the power of Excel, understanding its core terminology is vital.

Let's embark on a narrative journey through the landscape of Excel terms, where each concept will be illustrated through practical examples and anecdotes, making the language of Excel as familiar to you as your native tongue.

Cell: The fundamental building block of any Excel spreadsheet. Picture a cell as a single box in a vast grid, where each can hold a value, a formula, or text. For instance, imagine you're tracking monthly expenses; each expense amount occupies one cell in your spreadsheet. The cell is not just a static container; it dynamically calculates and updates values when formulas are applied.

Range: As you become more familiar with navigating spreadsheets, you'll often encounter the need to work with multiple cells simultaneously. A range in Excel is simply a collection of two or more cells. These cells can be contiguous, forming a block, or non-contiguous, scattered across the spreadsheet. Consider you have a list of daily sales figures throughout a month; highlighting all these cells from top to bottom forms a range. Operations can be performed on this range, like summing all the sales to get a monthly total.

Workbook and Worksheet: In the realm of Excel, these two terms are fundamental. A workbook is like the entire notebook containing numerous pages; each page represents a worksheet. You can have multiple worksheets within a single workbook, allowing you to organize various kinds of related data in one place. For example, a small business owner might have one worksheet for income, another for expenses, and a third for inventory, all within the same workbook.

Formula: The powerhouse of Excel, formulas are expressions used to calculate and process data. If you're calculating the total sales for a week, you'd sum up the daily sales figures using a formula like **=SUM(B1:B7)**, where **B1:B7** represents the range of sales from Monday to Sunday. Formulas in Excel begin with an equals sign (=), signaling Excel to perform a calculation.

Function: While formulas are manual calculations, functions are built-in shortcuts designed to carry out specific calculations. Each function in Excel has a specific purpose, such as **SUM()** for adding values, **AVERAGE()** for finding the mean, or **VLOOKUP()** for pulling data from a specific column. Using a function simplifies complex calculations, making your data work not only harder but smarter.

Row and Column: Rows run horizontally in an Excel sheet and are identified by numbers (1, 2, 3, ...). Columns run vertically and are labeled by letters (A, B, C, ...). This system of rows and columns creates an address system for each cell, where each cell can be identified by a column letter and a row number, such as A1, B25, or C300.

PivotTable: As you progress from basic data entry to more complex analysis, PivotTables become an invaluable tool. A PivotTable summarizes large amounts of data without the need for formulas. It's akin to summarizing a detailed book into a concise table of contents, where you can rearrange elements to highlight different aspects of the data.

Macro: For repetitive tasks, Excel offers macros—automated actions or sets of instructions that can be run whenever you need to perform the task. If you find yourself repeatedly formatting new data in the same way each week, a macro can automate this process, saving time and reducing potential errors.

Conditional Formatting: This feature allows cells to change their appearance based on the data they contain. For example, you might set a rule to highlight all expense cells greater than $500 in red. It's a visual aid that instantly draws attention to key figures and trends, allowing for quick analysis and decision-making.

Data Validation: Excel ensures data integrity through data validation, which restricts the type of data or the values that users can enter into a cell. For instance, you can set a cell to only accept dates before the current year or only numbers from a specified range. This tool is crucial in maintaining data accuracy and reliability.

Understanding these terms is not just about expanding your Excel vocabulary; it's about laying the foundation for all the tasks and operations you will perform. Each term is a tool in your toolkit, ready to be applied to a variety of data challenges. With these concepts mastered, you will find that Excel's language is not just one of numbers and formulas, but one of endless possibilities for efficiency, analysis, and insight. As we move forward in the guide, these terms will become second nature, enhancing your ability to transform raw data into actionable intelligence.

SETTING UP YOUR FIRST SPREADSHEET

Imagine you're setting up a new garden: you'd start by planning where each plant goes, considering what nutrients each needs, and how much space they require to thrive. Similarly, setting up your first spreadsheet in Excel 2024 involves understanding what you want to achieve, organizing your data logically, and ensuring each piece of data has the room to grow as insights and complexities develop.

Starting with a blank canvas, your first task is to open Excel 2024 and select a new blank workbook. This new workbook is pristine, full of potential and waiting for you to begin your data journey.

Naming Your Workbook

The first practical step in setting up your spreadsheet involves naming your workbook. Think of this as setting the title to your garden plan—it identifies what your project is about. You can save your workbook with a descriptive name that relates to its purpose, like 'Annual Sales Report 2024' or 'Employee Attendance Tracker'. This helps in organizing your documents and makes it easier to locate them later.

Begin by entering data into the cells. Click on a cell and start typing—whether it's text, numbers, or dates, Excel can handle various data types. If you're tracking expenses, for example, you might start by entering expense categories in the first column and dates in the first row. Remember, keeping data organized from the start sets you up for easier analysis later.

Adjusting Column Widths and Row Heights

As your data takes root, you might notice that some entries are cramped or spill over their cell boundaries. Adjusting column widths and row heights ensures that your data is readable and neat. Simply hover over the line between columns or rows in the header and drag to resize, or double-click to auto-fit the content precisely. This step is akin to spacing plants properly—you're giving each piece of data the room it needs to be clearly visible.

Formatting Cells

Applying basic formatting helps differentiate types of data visually and can make your spreadsheet easier to read. For instance, you could format header cells with a bold font and a different background color to distinguish them from data cells. Numbers can be formatted to display with two decimal places, and text alignments can be adjusted to enhance clarity.

To bring life to your data garden, you'll likely need to perform some calculations. Simple formulas in Excel are like the watering system for your garden—they make maintenance easier. For example, to sum expenses, you might enter **=SUM(B2:B10)** at the bottom of your column of numbers. Excel instantly calculates the total, updating it whenever the data changes.

Using Basic Functions

Excel's functions are pre-built formulas that simplify more complex calculations. For instance, the **AVERAGE()** function can be used to find the mean of a range of numbers, which is essential for quickly assessing performance metrics or financial outcomes.

Converting a range of data into a table provides several benefits, including easy formatting and sorting, the ability to filter data, and automatic updates when new data is added.

To create a table, select your range of data and choose **Insert > Table**. Once your data is in a table format, Excel provides options to add Total Rows, use slicers for filtering, and apply different styles for better readability.

Data Validation

To ensure that data entries are consistent and error-free, setting up data validation is crucial. For instance, if you only want to allow date entries in a specific format in a column, you can set up data validation to restrict inputs to that format. Go to **Data > Data Validation**, select the criteria, and define the input range. This is akin to putting up a fence in your garden—it guides where things should go and keeps out what doesn't belong.

After planting all your data seeds, remember to save your workbook. Regularly saving your progress prevents data loss and allows you to revert to earlier versions if needed.

Practice and Patience

Finally, like any garden, your Excel spreadsheet will grow and develop over time. It requires regular maintenance and adjustments as you add more data or as your needs change. Experiment with different features in Excel to see what works best for your particular dataset.

By following these steps to set up your first spreadsheet, you are not just organizing data; you are laying the groundwork for sophisticated analysis and insights that could influence key decisions in your professional landscape. Whether it's a simple list of household expenses or a complex annual budget, the principles remain the same: plan, plant, and cultivate your data carefully to reap the rewards of a well-maintained data garden.

2. BASIC OPERATIONS AND FORMATTING

ENTERING AND EDITING DATA

When you start using Excel 2024, entering and editing data is akin to sketching out the first few strokes on a canvas, setting the stage for the masterpiece to unfold. This process is fundamental, yet vital, ensuring that the groundwork is laid out meticulously to enable more complex operations and analyses later on.

Imagine you are creating a spreadsheet to manage a project. Each piece of data you enter is like placing a brick in the foundation of a building. You begin by opening a new sheet in your workbook, the blank grid in front of you ready to be filled with names, dates, tasks, and statuses.

Entering Data: The Basics

Entering data in Excel 2024 is straightforward: select a cell and begin typing. Press **Enter**, and the cursor moves down to the next row, ready for more input. This intuitive navigation makes it easy to move quickly through a list. If you're inputting data horizontally, pressing **Tab** after each entry shifts the cursor to the right. It's a rhythmic motion, almost musical, as you tab and type, tab and type, filling the rows and columns with valuable data.

As your project management spreadsheet begins to take shape, you'll enter data such as the task name in column A, the responsible party in column B, the due date in column C, and the status in column D. The act of entering this data can be done manually, but Excel also supports more efficient methods:

- **Copy and Paste:** Excel's versatility allows you to copy data from another source, such as a web page or a different spreadsheet, and paste it directly into your workbook. This is especially useful when dealing with large datasets.
- **Drag and Fill:** For data that follows a pattern or sequence, Excel's fill handle allows you to automatically fill cells. Simply type the beginning of a sequence, select the cell, then drag the fill handle (a small square at the bottom-right corner of the cell) across the cells you want to fill.

Editing and Updating Data

Once data is entered, editing is inevitable as project parameters change or more accurate information becomes available. Clicking on a cell allows you to type directly over the previous entry, but Excel offers even more refined editing tools:

- **Formula Bar:** Located above the column headers, the formula bar displays the contents of the selected cell and allows you to make edits directly, especially useful for longer text entries or formulas.
- **Find and Replace:** When changes are extensive, such as updating the name of a project contributor throughout the spreadsheet, the **Find and Replace** feature can update all instances simultaneously, ensuring consistency and saving time.

Formatting Cells for Data Entry

Data in Excel isn't just about numbers and text; it's about presenting this information in a readable and understandable form. Formatting plays a critical role:

- **Number Formatting:** Right-clicking a cell or range of cells and selecting **Format Cells** brings up options to format data as currency, date, percentage, and more. For instance, formatting a column where financial figures are entered as currency standardizes the data presentation and automatically applies decimal places.
- **Text Formatting:** Adjusting the font size, style, and color not only makes your spreadsheet aesthetically pleasing but also organizes and differentiates between types of data, such as using bold text for headings or different colors for different statuses in a project management tool.

Utilizing Excel's Data Validation

To ensure that data entered into your spreadsheet adheres to specific criteria, Excel's **Data Validation** feature is essential. It restricts what can be entered into a cell—such as preventing a date of birth in the future or a budget entry exceeding a certain amount. This tool helps maintain the integrity and accuracy of your data, acting as a gatekeeper to ensure only valid data is stored.

- **Setting up Data Validation:** You might restrict a column to only contain dates within a particular range or a list of values (e.g., "Completed," "In Progress," "Not Started") to standardize entries.

The Art of Data Entry

Entering and editing data in Excel 2024, although fundamentally simple, carries with it the weight of ensuring accuracy and efficiency in data manipulation and analysis. Each cell filled, each number formatted, and each validation set contributes to a robust, reliable database that supports your objectives, whether managing a complex project or tracking personal expenses.

With these skills honed, the data you compile will not only be a collection of names, numbers, and dates but a well-oiled machine ready to perform complex operations, analyze trends, and inform decisions with precision. As you progress through your Excel journey, remember that the art of data entry is your stepping stone to mastering this powerful tool, enabling you to capture and harness the potential of every piece of information effectively.

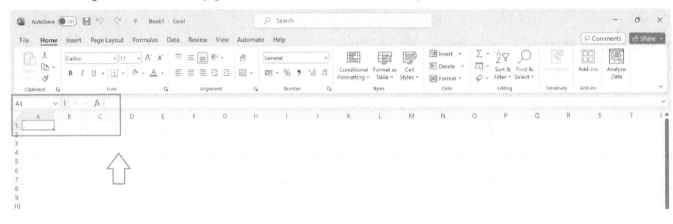

NUMBER FORMATTING TECHNIQUES

In the intricate dance of data management within Excel 2024, understanding how to adeptly manipulate number formatting is akin to mastering the steps of a sophisticated ballroom dance. Each step, turn, and flourish adds clarity and precision to the numerical data, enhancing both its appearance and functionality. Let us delve into the nuances of number formatting in Excel, exploring how each technique can transform raw data into clear, actionable information that drives decision-making.

Imagine you are preparing a financial report. The raw numbers spill across your spreadsheet—revenues, expenses, percentages, dates. Your first task is to transform these figures into a format that is immediately understandable and visually digestible. This is where Excel's robust number formatting capabilities come into play, ensuring that each figure conveys the right message at a glance.

Basic Number Formatting

The simplest form of number formatting might involve converting a string of digits into a currency format or adjusting the decimal places to standardize financial data. To apply a basic number format:

1. Select the cells you wish to format.
2. Right-click and choose 'Format Cells', or use the shortcut Ctrl+1.
3. In the Format Cells dialog box, navigate to the 'Number' tab.
4. Choose your desired format from the list provided—Currency, Accounting, Date, Percentage, etc.

For example, selecting 'Currency' will format your numbers with a dollar sign, two decimal places, and commas as thousand separators. This instantly transforms a raw number like **12345.6** into **$12,345.60**, making it clear that you are dealing with a monetary amount.

Custom Number Formatting

Beyond basic formatting, Excel allows you to dive deeper with custom formats. This feature lets you tailor data presentation to your exact needs, whether you're adjusting visual layout, adding text or symbols, or changing color based on conditions.

To create a custom format:

1. Follow the same steps to open the Format Cells dialog.
2. Select 'Custom' from the category list.
3. In the 'Type' box, input your custom format code.

Here, the possibilities broaden. For example, you can format a number to appear with a specific number of decimal places, or include text in your format. Entering **0.00 "Kg"** as a custom format will display the number **5** as **5.00 Kg**, integrating units directly into the data cell.

Conditional Formatting

Conditional formatting takes number formatting to a dynamic level, where data can automatically change appearance based on specified conditions. This is particularly useful for quickly highlighting trends, outliers, or critical values in a dataset.

To apply conditional formatting:

1. Select the cells you want to format.
2. Go to the 'Home' tab.
3. Click 'Conditional Formatting'.
4. Choose a rule from the dropdown menus, such as 'Highlight Cell Rules' or 'Data Bars'.

For instance, setting up a rule to highlight all values above **10,000** in red can immediately draw attention to higher figures in a sales report. Excel 2024 provides a range of pre-set conditions but also allows for custom rule creation, giving you flexibility in how data responds to the conditions you set.

Formatting Dates and Times

Dates and times in Excel can be particularly tricky due to their unique formatting requirements. Excel stores dates as serial numbers; thus, formatting is essential to make them comprehensible. To format dates and times:

1. Select your date or time cells.
2. Open the Format Cells dialog.
3. Choose 'Date' or 'Time' from the category and select the format that suits your data presentation needs.

Choosing the right date format might mean the difference between displaying **4/7/2024**, **July 4, 2024**, or **Saturday, July 4, 2024**. Each option serves different purposes, from concise reporting to detailed event planning.

Utilizing Formatting for Data Analysis

The strategic use of number formatting can significantly enhance data analysis. For instance, applying different color codes to specific ranges of numbers can provide visual cues about data distribution. Formatting negative numbers in red (using the custom format **0.00;[Red]-0.00**) immediately flags losses in a financial statement, allowing quicker reaction and decision-making. In essence, number formatting in Excel is not just about making data pretty; it's about making it practical, comprehensible, and actionable. Whether you are preparing a report, analyzing trends, or just keeping track of personal data, the way you format your numbers can profoundly impact the readability and effectiveness of your spreadsheet. As you become more familiar with these techniques, you will find that your spreadsheets are not only more accurate but also more persuasive, driving home the points that matter most in your data narrative.

WORKING WITH TEXT AND DATES

Working with text and dates in Excel 2024 is an essential skill, akin to knowing how to navigate the intricacies of a new language or mastering the timing of a complex recipe. Text and dates are fundamental data types that you will manipulate in Excel, each with its unique set of functions and challenges.

As you learn to effectively handle these elements, you'll find yourself able to communicate more clearly and manage timelines more efficiently, enhancing both the usability and accuracy of your spreadsheets.

Mastering Text Functions

Excel is not just about numbers and formulas; it's also a powerful tool for manipulating text. Whether you're organizing data, extracting specific information, or formatting entries for consistency, understanding how to use Excel's text functions can significantly streamline your workflow.

- **Concatenate:** This function is like a binding glue for text. It combines two or more text strings into one. For example, if you have first names in one column and last names in another, you can use **=CONCATENATE(A1, " ", B1)** to merge them into a full name with a space in between.

- **Proper, Upper, Lower:** These functions adjust the text casing. **=PROPER(A1)** converts text to title case (capitalizing the first letter of each word), **=UPPER(A1)** converts text to all uppercase, and **=LOWER(A1)** makes all letters lowercase. Such functions are invaluable when you need to standardize text data for reports or data entry.

- **Left, Right, Mid:** These string functions extract sub-strings from a larger string based on the number of characters you specify. **=LEFT(A1, 4)** extracts the first four characters from the left of the text in cell A1, useful for tasks like extracting an area code from a phone number.

- **Trim:** When working with data that has been imported from other sources, you often encounter extra spaces that can affect sorting and searching functions. **=TRIM(A1)** removes unnecessary spaces from text except for single spaces between words.

- **Find, Search:** These functions locate the position of one text string within another, which can be useful for sorting or categorizing entries based on specific criteria. **=SEARCH("dog", A1)** would give you the starting position of the word "dog" within the cell A1.

Navigating Dates

Dates in Excel are formatted as serial numbers, allowing you to perform calculations on them just as you would with other numerical data. However, dates also come with their own set of functions that enable you to extract specific parts of a date or calculate durations.

- **Today, Now:** =TODAY() inserts the current date into a cell, while =NOW() inserts the current date and time. These functions are useful for creating timestamps or calculating ages and durations.
- **Year, Month, Day:** These functions pull out the respective part of a date. For example, =YEAR(A1) would return the year from the date in cell A1. This can be particularly useful for sorting or grouping data by month or year.
- **DateDif:** This function is a workhorse for calculating the difference between two dates. =DATEDIF(A1, B1, "d") calculates the number of days between two dates listed in cells A1 and B1. You can change the "d" to "m" for months or "y" for years, depending on your needs.
- **EOMonth:** This function returns the last day of the month a specified number of months before or after a given date. For example, =EOMONTH(A1, 1) will give you the date of the end of the month one month after the date in cell A1.

Formatting Dates and Text

Proper formatting of text and dates not only improves the readability of your data but also ensures that Excel can interpret and calculate it correctly.

- **Text Formatting:** Excel offers a range of options to format text data, including font type, size, color, and text alignment. These can be accessed from the Home tab under the Font group.
- **Date Formatting:** Similarly, Excel allows you to choose from various date formats or create custom formats to suit your needs. This ensures that dates are displayed in a way that is most meaningful for your specific context.

Understanding and utilizing these functions and formatting options for text and dates will equip you to handle a wide range of data types effectively. From organizing contact lists to managing project timelines, mastering these skills will not only save you time but also prevent common data errors. As you continue to explore Excel 2024, remember that each text string you format correctly and every date you calculate accurately builds towards greater confidence and competence in handling all the data challenges that come your way.

3. CREATING YOUR FIRST FORMULAS

UNDERSTANDING CELL REFERENCES

Understanding cell references in Excel 2024 is akin to mastering the coordinates of a map; it's about knowing exactly where you are and where you need to go. This foundational knowledge is crucial because it supports everything from basic data entry to the construction of complex, dynamic formulas that automatically update as your data changes. As you embark on this journey into the heart of Excel's functionality, it's essential to grasp the nuances of cell references to leverage the full potential of your data manipulation skills.

What are Cell References?

At its simplest, a cell reference identifies a cell's location in the spreadsheet through a combination of letters and numbers. The letter represents the column while the number signifies the row. For example, B3 refers to the cell located at the intersection of column B and row 3.

Types of Cell References

Relative References

Imagine you're giving directions that say "two blocks north of the bakery." This direction changes based on your starting point, similar to how relative references change when you copy them across your spreadsheet. If you use a formula like **=A1+10** in cell B1 and then drag that formula down to B2, it automatically adjusts to **=A2+10**. This is because the reference is relative to the position where it's copied.

Absolute References

Now, consider a landmark that doesn't change, like the Empire State Building. Directions given in relation to this landmark always point to the same place, much like absolute references in Excel. By placing a dollar sign before the column letter and/or the row number, you fix the reference point. For example, **$A$1** is an absolute reference. No matter where you copy the formula **=$A$1+10**, it always refers to cell A1.

Mixed References

A mixed reference is a blend of both relative and absolute references, like giving directions using one fixed point and one variable point. For example, **$A1** fixes the column but allows the row reference to adjust. This type of reference is incredibly useful for formulas that need to iterate over rows but stay in the same column or vice versa.

Practical Applications of Cell References

Building a Monthly Expense Table

Imagine setting up a table where you want to calculate the expenses for each month. You could place the monthly expenses in cells B2 through B13 and a percentage tax rate in cell C1. To calculate the tax for each month in column C, you could use the formula **=B2*$C$1** in cell C2 and drag it down through C13. The dollar sign in **$C$1** ensures that as you drag the formula down, it continues to reference the tax rate correctly, even though the reference to the expenses changes relative to the row.

Dynamic Data Ranges

When analyzing data that regularly updates, such as a sales record, using relative references allows your calculations to adjust automatically as new data is added. If you're totaling sales in column A, the formula **=SUM(A1:A10)** could be expanded automatically by dragging the fill handle down as new sales data is entered into subsequent rows.

Creating Robust Formulas

Understanding and using different types of cell references allow you to build more robust formulas. Suppose you are preparing a financial model where certain constants (like tax rates or currency conversion rates) need to remain fixed regardless of where the formula is applied within the spreadsheet. Using absolute or mixed references can ensure these elements remain unchanged, which is critical for maintaining the accuracy of your computations.

Tips for Managing Cell References

- **Use Names for Cell References**: Naming a cell or a range of cells can simplify your formulas and make them easier to understand. For example, naming cell C1 as "TaxRate" allows you to use **=B2*TaxRate** instead of **=B2*$C$1**, making the formula more readable.

- **Check for Errors**: When copying formulas, it's easy to make mistakes with cell references. Always double-check that the references in your formulas are pointing to the correct cells, especially when using relative references.
- **Leverage the Trace Precedents and Dependents Tools**: Excel offers tools to trace the cells that affect the active cell's value (precedents) and the cells affected by the active cell (dependents). These tools are invaluable for debugging complex formulas.

Mastering cell references is about more than just learning Excel mechanics—it's about thinking strategically to set up your spreadsheets for easy updates and accurate analysis. By understanding and applying different types of cell references effectively, you ensure that your data not only remains reliable but also dynamic, adjusting seamlessly as your data grows and evolves.

BASIC MATHEMATICAL FUNCTIONS

Excel 2024 is not just a platform for managing data; it is a powerful tool for performing mathematical operations that can transform raw data into insightful information. Whether you are tallying up expenses, calculating sales increases, or estimating project timelines, understanding how to use Excel's basic mathematical functions is essential. These functions serve as the building blocks for more complex data analysis tasks, providing you with the tools you need to make informed decisions based on quantitative data.

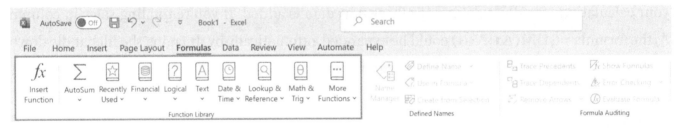

Exploring the Basic Mathematical Functions

Excel offers a suite of basic mathematical functions that include addition, subtraction, multiplication, and division—each of which plays a critical role in daily data operations.

- **Addition (+)**: The simplest of all, addition involves summing numbers together. For example, if you want to calculate the total cost of items purchased, you would use the **SUM** function, such as **=SUM(A1:A5)** to add up all values from cell A1 to A5.
- **Subtraction (-)**: Subtraction is used to determine the difference between two numbers. If you need to calculate the remaining budget after some expenses, you would subtract the total expenses from your initial budget, e.g., **=B1-C1** where B1 is your budget and C1 is the expenses.

- **Multiplication (*)**: Multiplication is used when you need to calculate the total impact of multiple units, such as determining total sales when you know the quantity sold and the price per unit, e.g., **=A2*B2**.
- **Division (/)**: Division is used to distribute a total into parts or to compare the sizes of two quantities, such as calculating the average cost per item if you divide the total cost by the number of items, e.g., **=A1/B1**.

These basic functions are frequently used not only as standalone operations but also as part of more complex formulas where multiple operations are combined to yield a final result.

Applying Functions to Real-World Scenarios

Imagine you are managing a project and need to keep track of various metrics, such as cost, time, and resource allocation. Here's how you might apply Excel's basic mathematical functions:

- **Project Budgeting**: To manage your project's budget, you might sum up all individual expense items using the **SUM** function to see the total expenditure. Further, to find out how much each team member has spent versus the average, you might subtract individual expenses from the average or even use division to see each member's spending as a percentage of the total.
- **Resource Allocation**: If each unit of work requires a certain number of hours and you know the total hours available from each team member, multiplication can help you calculate the total units of work that can be handled by each team member.
- **Performance Metrics**: To evaluate performance metrics, such as sales per day, you could divide the total sales by the number of days to get an average, helping you understand daily performance trends.

Best Practices for Using Mathematical Functions

To ensure accuracy and efficiency when using mathematical functions in Excel, consider the following best practices:

- **Precision**: Always ensure that the cells you are referencing contain the correct data types. Numeric operations on cells containing text or improperly formatted data can lead to errors or misleading results.
- **Clarity**: Keep your formulas as simple and clear as possible. Complex formulas can be powerful, but they can also be difficult to troubleshoot if errors arise. Using intermediate cells to hold calculations can help keep your main formulas straightforward.

- **Verification**: After setting up your formulas, verify them by manually checking the results of a few calculations. This step is crucial to ensure that your formulas are working correctly before relying on their outputs for decision-making.
- **Documentation**: Document your formulas within your spreadsheet, either through comments or a separate documentation sheet. This practice is especially important in collaborative environments to help others understand how your calculations are structured.

Excel's basic mathematical functions are like the primary colors from which you can mix an infinite array of shades. Each function might seem simple on its own, but when combined effectively, they can help you paint detailed and comprehensive pictures of your data landscape. Whether you are a novice learning to navigate the basics or a seasoned professional refining your analytical skills, these functions are essential tools in your Excel toolkit, enabling you to turn data into actionable insights.

COPYING AND PASTING FORMULAS

Imagine you've just painted a small section of a mural with a combination of colors and patterns that perfectly convey your vision. Now, you want to replicate that exact blend throughout the entire wall without losing any detail or vibrancy in each repetition. In Excel 2024, copying and pasting formulas allows you to do just that with your data, maintaining the integrity of your calculations while extending them across different segments of your spreadsheet.

The Basics of Copying and Pasting Formulas

Copying and pasting formulas in Excel is foundational yet powerful. It enables you to apply the same calculation across multiple rows or columns without manually re-entering the formula. This capability not only saves time but also ensures accuracy and consistency in your data processing. When you copy a formula, Excel automatically adjusts the cell references, assuming you want them to relate dynamically to their new location. This feature, known as relative referencing, can be incredibly useful but also a source of confusion if not properly understood.

Step-by-Step: How to Copy and Paste Formulas

1. **Select the Cell**: Click on the cell that contains the formula you want to copy.
2. **Copy the Formula**: You can copy the formula by right-clicking and selecting "Copy," or by pressing **Ctrl+C** on your keyboard.
3. **Select the Destination**: Click on the cell or range of cells where you want this formula to be applied.

4. **Paste the Formula**: Right-click and select one of the paste options, or press **Ctrl+V**.

Understanding Paste Options

Excel 2024 offers several paste options that cater to different needs:

- **Formulas**: This option pastes the formulas along with their relative references.
- **Values**: Instead of pasting the formula, Excel will calculate the formula in the original cell and paste the resulting value.
- **Formulas and Number Formatting**: This pastes the formula and any formatting that was applied to the original cell.
- **Transpose**: This option allows you to switch data from rows to columns or vice versa while pasting.

These options provide flexibility depending on whether you need the raw data, the calculations, or the exact styling from the original cell.

Special Considerations When Copying Formulas

Absolute References

Sometimes, you don't want Excel to adjust cell references when copying formulas. This is where absolute references (using the **$** symbol, like **$A$1**) become crucial. If your original formula was meant to always refer to a specific cell, converting the cell reference to absolute ensures that copying the formula doesn't change this reference.

Using the Fill Handle

For efficient data entry, Excel's fill handle is a valuable tool. It's a small square at the bottom-right corner of the selected cell. When you drag the fill handle across other cells, Excel copies the formula from the first cell into the others, automatically adjusting the cell references based on relative positioning.

Dragging Formulas Across Rows and Columns

Dragging formulas using the fill handle can behave differently depending on whether you drag vertically or horizontally. This behavior is particularly important to watch when your formulas involve both row and column references.

Common Pitfalls and How to Avoid Them

While copying and pasting formulas can streamline your workflow, it can also lead to errors if not done thoughtfully. Here are a few tips to ensure you maintain data integrity:

- **Check Your References**: After copying a formula, always check a few of the resulting cells to ensure the references were adjusted correctly.

- **Watch for #REF! Errors**: These errors occur when you copy a formula that refers to cells that don't exist in the paste area. Always ensure that your paste area is appropriate for the formula.

- **Lock Important References**: If a formula should always refer to a specific cell or range, use absolute references to prevent unwanted changes when copying and pasting.

Copying and pasting formulas is more than just a technical task; it's an art form that requires attention to detail and an understanding of your data's landscape. By mastering this skill, you enhance your ability to manage large datasets efficiently, allowing you to replicate calculations accurately across your entire data set, much like a painter ensuring every part of the mural reflects their artistic intent. This skill ensures that as your spreadsheet grows, your data remains robust and your analyses sharp.

4. DATA MANAGEMENT ESSENTIALS

SORTING AND FILTERING DATA

In the realm of data management, sorting and filtering stand out as two of the most fundamental yet powerful techniques available in Excel 2024. They are the tools that transform a chaotic jumble of data into orderly, understandable information. Just as a librarian organizes books to make finding a particular volume quick and easy, sorting and filtering in Excel help you organize and surface the data you need to see.

Understanding Sorting

Sorting data is the process of arranging it in a meaningful order to facilitate easier analysis. You can sort data alphabetically, numerically, or even chronologically, depending on the nature of the data involved.

How to Sort Data

To sort data in Excel 2024:

1. Select the range of data you want to sort. If your data is in a table format, Excel automatically recognizes its extent.
2. Navigate to the **Data** tab on the Ribbon.
3. Choose **Sort A to Z** or **Sort Z to A** for a quick sort. For a more customized sorting:
   - Click on **Sort** to open the sorting dialog box.
   - You can specify the column to sort by and choose whether the sort should be ascending or descending.
   - Excel also allows you to add multiple levels of sorting criteria, enabling you to sort by one column and then by another, a useful feature when dealing with complex datasets.

Sorting is particularly helpful when you need to organize data into a logical sequence—for instance, sorting a list of employees by surname or a series of dates in a project timeline.

Exploring Filtering

Filtering data allows you to display only the rows that meet certain criteria while temporarily hiding the others. It enables you to focus on specific segments of your data without being distracted by irrelevant information.

How to Filter Data

To apply filters in Excel 2024:

1. Select your data range or click anywhere within your data table.
2. Go to the **Data** tab and click on **Filter**. This will toggle dropdown arrows in the header row.
3. Click on the dropdown arrow in the column header that you want to filter by.
4. A checklist appears showing all the unique items in that column. You can select or deselect items to show or hide them.
5. For more complex filtering, you can use criteria such as "greater than," "less than," or "between" to filter numerical data, or text filters to work with text data.

Filters are extremely useful when you need to analyze subsets of data—such as viewing all sales transactions that exceed a certain value, or all inventory items in a specific category.

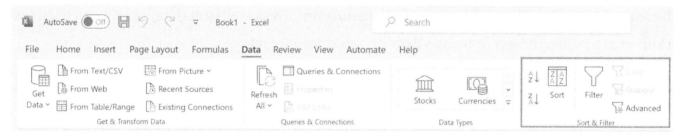

Practical Applications of Sorting and Filtering

Imagine you are handling a dataset containing sales information from multiple regions. You might:

- **Sort** the data by region and then by sales amount to understand which areas are performing best.
- **Filter** the data to show only those transactions that occurred in the last quarter, or only those that exceed a certain dollar amount, focusing your analysis on the most relevant facts.

Best Practices for Sorting and Filtering

When managing your data with sorting and filtering, consider the following tips:

- **Maintain clean headers**: Ensure that each column has a unique and descriptive header. This simplifies the process of applying filters and understanding what each column represents.
- **Check for merged cells**: Sorting does not work well with merged cells in the range you want to sort. Before sorting, make sure to unmerge any cells or modify your data layout to avoid merged cells in your data tables.

- **Use Tables**: Converting your data range into a table (Insert > Table) can enhance both sorting and filtering. Tables offer dynamic ranges that automatically adjust as your data changes, which is particularly helpful when regularly adding new data.

Automating with Advanced Filter

For more advanced scenarios, Excel's **Advanced Filter** can be a powerful tool. It allows you to set up complex criteria to filter your data, which can be beneficial when you need to apply multiple conditions. For instance, using an advanced filter, you could display all records where the sales are above a certain amount and the product is within a specific category.

Sorting and filtering in Excel are not merely about managing data; they are about setting the stage for deeper insights and more effective decision-making. By mastering these tools, you turn the overwhelming sea of data into a navigable waterway, guiding you to the valuable insights that lie beneath the surface. This ability to quickly organize and access relevant data is not just a technical skill—it is a strategic asset in today's data-driven environment.

INTRODUCTION TO TABLES

Excel 2024 elevates the art of data management by enhancing the functionality of tables, transforming how we organize, analyze, and present data. Think of a table in Excel not just as a collection of rows and columns, but as a dynamic structure designed to make your data more accessible and easier to manipulate. It's akin to having an intelligent data assistant who knows precisely how to arrange your information for maximum efficiency and clarity.

The Essence of Excel Tables

Using tables in Excel 2024 is about harnessing a powerful set of tools that streamline the handling of data sets, making operations like sorting, filtering, calculating, and visualizing much simpler and more efficient. Tables are particularly useful because they allow you to manage and analyze related groups of data independently of other data in the worksheet.

Creating a Table

To begin with, any range of cells containing data can be transformed into a table:

1. Select the range of data you want to turn into a table.
2. Navigate to the **Insert** tab on the Ribbon and click on **Table**, or use the shortcut **Ctrl+T**.
3. Excel will automatically detect the range for the table if you have selected your data range. Ensure the **My table has headers** option is checked if your data includes headers.

4. Click **OK**, and your data range will now be formatted as a table with Excel's default style.

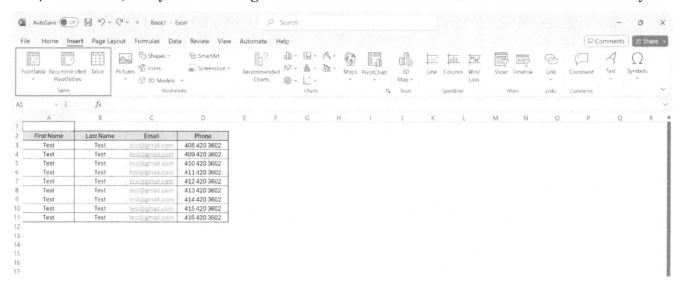

Benefits of Using Tables

Tables in Excel are not merely about aesthetic formatting; they provide a structured framework that offers several benefits:

- **Structured References**: When you create formulas within a table, Excel uses structured references that are easier to understand than traditional cell addresses. For example, instead of using **A2**, the formula might refer to **@[Sales]**, indicating it's using the Sales column in the current row.

- **Auto Expansion**: Tables automatically expand to include additional data when you enter new data adjacent to them. This auto-expansion makes it easy to add or remove data without manually adjusting range references in your formulas.

- **Built-in Tools for Data Management**: Tables come with their own set of tools and options, such as built-in filters and a designated tab on the Ribbon that appears when you work within a table. These tools make it straightforward to sort, filter, and process data directly within the table.

Practical Scenarios for Tables

Tables are particularly valuable in scenarios where data is continuously updated and needs frequent analysis:

- **Financial Analysis**: Imagine managing monthly financial statements. A table can help streamline the process of updating figures, calculating totals, or averages, and comparing monthly changes using formulas that automatically adjust to the changing data.

- **Inventory Management**: For an inventory sheet, a table format allows for easy additions and updates of stock levels, automatic recalculations of totals, and quick sorting and filtering based on categories like stock levels, categories, or due dates.

Customizing Tables

Excel 2024 offers extensive customization options to enhance the functionality and appearance of tables:

- **Style Options**: You can change the look of your table by choosing from various predefined styles or creating your own to match your organization's or project's theme.
- **Calculated Columns**: When you enter a formula in one cell in a column within a table, Excel will automatically fill the same formula in all other cells in that column, using relative references specific to each row.
- **Slicers**: For more interactive filtering, you can insert slicers connected to your table. Slicers provide buttons that you can click to filter table data based on criteria, making it much easier to manage large sets of data visually.

Best Practices for Table Management

To maximize the effectiveness of tables in Excel 2024, consider the following best practices:

- **Keep Headers Clear and Concise**: Ensure your table headers accurately describe the data they contain. This clarity is crucial when using features like structured references, as it helps keep your formulas intelligible.
- **Avoid Blank Rows and Columns**: Tables work best when they are contiguous blocks of data. Blank rows and columns can disrupt functions like sorting and filtering and can cause issues with formulas.
- **Regularly Update and Review Table Settings**: As your needs change, so too should your tables. Regularly review your table settings and structures to ensure they still serve your intended purpose, especially when dealing with dynamic and evolving data sets.

Incorporating tables into your Excel workflow is about more than organizing data—it's about enhancing your overall data interaction experience. With tables, Excel 2024 not only simplifies data management tasks but also significantly boosts your productivity and data analysis capabilities. As you become more familiar with these tools, you'll discover that tables are indispensable for managing complex information, providing a solid foundation for your data-driven decisions.

DATA VALIDATION TECHNIQUES

In the digital age, data is not only abundant but also pivotal to decision-making in business, science, and many other fields. Ensuring the integrity of this data through meticulous validation processes in Excel 2024 is akin to a chef ensuring the freshness of ingredients before preparing a meal—essential for the best results. Data validation in Excel 2024 involves setting specific rules that dictate what data can or cannot be entered into a cell, thus maintaining the accuracy and reliability of your datasets.

Understanding Data Validation

Data validation is used to control the type of data or the values that users can enter into a cell. For example, you might want to restrict entries in a cell to certain numbers, dates, or a list from a drop-down menu to prevent data entry errors.

This feature is particularly useful in scenarios like inventory management, budgeting, or any form of data gathering where specific input criteria are required.

Implementing Data Validation in Excel 2024

To start using data validation in Excel 2024, you'll follow several steps to set up restrictions and rules that help guide data entry:

1. **Select the Cells**: Begin by selecting the cells or range where you want to apply data validation.
2. **Access the Data Validation Tool**:
   - Navigate to the **Data** tab on the Ribbon.
   - Click on **Data Validation** in the 'Data Tools' group.
   - This opens the Data Validation dialog box, where you can set the criteria for data entry.
3. **Setting Validation Criteria**:
   - In the **Settings** tab, under the **Allow** dropdown menu, select the type of data you want to permit, such as whole numbers, decimal, list, date, time, text length, or custom.
   - Depending on your selection, additional options will be available to specify further, like setting a range of valid numbers or dates, or a list of acceptable entries.
4. **Creating Drop-Down Lists**:
   - One common validation technique is to create a drop-down list that limits entries to predefined options.

- Choose 'List' from the **Allow** dropdown, then enter the values directly in the **Source** box, separated by commas, or reference a range on the spreadsheet where the valid options are listed.

5. **Custom Formulas in Validation**:
   - For complex conditions that can't be defined by standard options, use the **Custom** option in the validation criteria.
   - Enter a formula that returns TRUE for valid entries and FALSE for invalid ones. For instance, to ensure a number is not only positive but also less than a certain value, you might use a formula like **=AND(A1>0, A1<100)**.

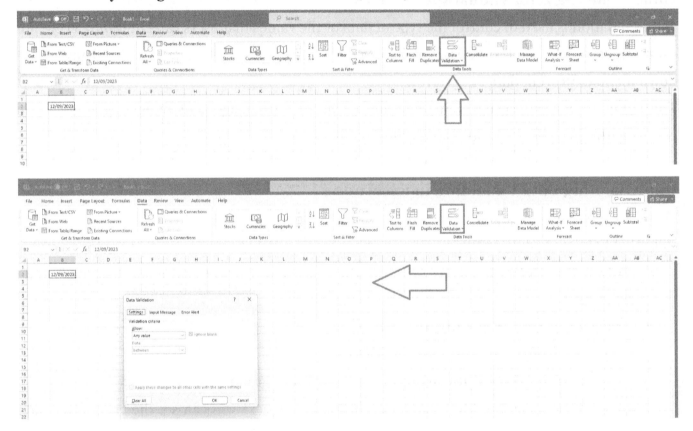

Managing Validation Feedback

A critical aspect of data validation is providing feedback to help guide users who are entering data:

- **Input Message**: You can set an input message that appears when the cell is selected, informing the user of the validation requirement. This is akin to a gentle reminder of what should be entered.
- **Error Alert**: If invalid data is entered, you can configure Excel to show an error alert. You can choose the style of the alert (stop, warning, information) and customize the title and the message text to make it as informative as possible.

Practical Applications and Tips

Consider a scenario where you are managing registration for an event and need to capture participant information:

- **Use lists for standardized inputs** such as shirt sizes or states to ensure data uniformity.
- **Employ date validations** to prevent entries of unrealistic or erroneous dates.
- **Utilize custom formulas** to validate complex conditions, like checking if a participant's reported age corresponds logically with their birthdate.

Best Practices for Data Validation

- **Combine Validation with Conditional Formatting**: To make it even clearer which cells have validation applied, use conditional formatting to change the appearance of these cells.
- **Regularly Update Validation Criteria**: As requirements change, make sure to update your validation rules to match new criteria.
- **Document Your Validation Rules**: For spreadsheets that will be used by others, document the validation rules applied and any relevant formulas. This documentation can be crucial for maintenance or for troubleshooting by others.

Data validation in Excel 2024 is a powerful ally in ensuring that the data you gather is accurate and suitable for analysis. By carefully setting up and managing validation rules, you ensure that your Excel workbooks not only capture data efficiently but do so in a way that maintains quality and consistency, ultimately making your data-driven decisions as reliable as possible.

PART II: MASTERING DATA ANALYSIS TOOLS

5. DIVE INTO DATA ANALYSIS

ADVANCED FILTERING OPTIONS

As we delve deeper into the capabilities of Excel 2024, advanced filtering emerges as a crucial technique in the data analyst's toolkit. This powerful feature goes beyond simple data sorting and querying; it allows for sophisticated data manipulation and extraction, facilitating detailed analysis and insights from large datasets. Imagine you are an archaeologist sifting through layers of earth to uncover hidden artifacts. Advanced filtering in Excel provides the tools to sift through layers of data to reveal the critical information beneath.

Introduction to Advanced Filtering

Advanced filtering in Excel is about applying complex criteria to refine your data dynamically. While basic filtering lets you quickly sort data based on standard parameters, advanced filtering can combine conditions, apply formulas, and even use external data ranges to precisely control what data appears.

Setting Up Advanced Filters

To initiate an advanced filter:

1. **Prepare Your Data**: Ensure your dataset includes clear, concise headers. Advanced filtering relies on header labels to apply criteria correctly.
2. **Define Criteria Range**: Set up a separate area in your worksheet where you specify the criteria for filtering your data. This range should include one or more header labels from your data set and the conditions for filtering under these headers.
3. **Apply the Filter**:
   - Navigate to the **Data** tab and select **Advanced** in the Sort & Filter group.
   - In the dialog box that appears, specify your list range (your data), your criteria range, and decide whether to filter the list in place or to copy to another location.

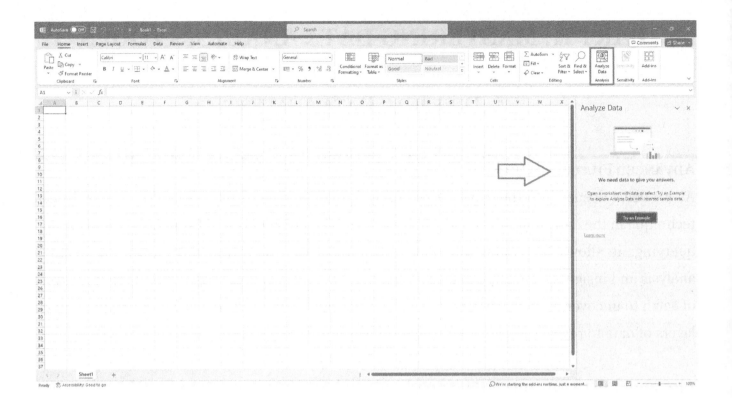

Criteria Range Examples

You might use criteria such as:

- Multiple conditions in one column (e.g., dates after **01/01/2024** AND before **12/31/2024**).
- Conditions across multiple columns (e.g., sales greater than $5000 in **Region A**).
- Use wildcards for partial text matches (e.g., names that start with "J").

Leveraging Formulas in Filters

One of the most powerful aspects of advanced filtering is the ability to use formulas to set criteria. This method provides flexibility beyond fixed criteria, allowing for dynamic conditions based on calculations.

- **Formula-Based Criteria**: For instance, to filter records where the sales tax has not been calculated (assuming a tax rate of 5%), you might use a formula like **=B2*0.05 <> C2** where column B is sales and column C is the sales tax charged. The filter will then show only those records where the calculated tax does not match the charged tax.

Practical Applications

Consider a scenario in a retail business where you need to analyze customer purchases to determine patterns:

- **Seasonal Trends**: Set criteria to filter data for different seasons and compare year-over-year changes.
- **Customer Segmentation**: Filter data to see purchasing behaviors among different customer demographics.
- **Product Performance**: Use advanced filters to isolate data for specific products or categories to analyze sales performance.

Best Practices for Advanced Filtering

To maximize the effectiveness and accuracy of your advanced filtering efforts, consider the following tips:

- **Data Consistency**: Ensure your data is consistently formatted, as advanced filtering is sensitive to data types and inconsistencies can lead to erroneous or unexpected results.
- **Clear Criteria Definitions**: Make your criteria range easy to understand and modify. This can be particularly important when sharing your work with others or when you need to adjust criteria frequently.
- **Documentation**: Keep a record of the criteria used in your filters, especially when using complex formulas. This documentation is invaluable for troubleshooting and review purposes.

With the introduction of dynamic arrays in Excel 2024, advanced filtering can be combined with array formulas to automate and expand data analysis tasks. For instance, you can filter data and automatically populate arrays that feed into dashboards or reports, streamlining the process of updating key metrics.

Advanced filtering in Excel 2024 is a testament to the software's deep capabilities in handling and analyzing data. By mastering these techniques, you equip yourself with the skills to not only manage large volumes of data but also to extract meaningful insights that can influence decision-making and strategic planning. Like the finely tuned instruments of a skilled musician, advanced filtering techniques allow you to orchestrate data in ways that reveal new patterns, trends, and opportunities, turning raw data into actionable intelligence.

USING CONDITIONAL FORMATTING

In the landscape of Excel 2024, where data not only informs but drives decision-making, conditional formatting stands out as a beacon, guiding users through seas of numbers by highlighting what's important. Just as a lighthouse illuminates hazards to navigation, conditional formatting uses colors, gradients, and icons to point out critical data points, trends, and exceptions. This feature enhances the usability and readability of complex data sets by allowing you to visually emphasize differences in the data and identify patterns and trends quickly.

What is Conditional Formatting?

Conditional formatting in Excel allows you to apply specific formatting—like changing the color of a cell—based on the data it contains. Essentially, it lets you create visual distinctions by applying color scales, icon sets, and other graphical annotations to your data, depending on the value of cells.

Setting Up Conditional Formatting

To apply conditional formatting in Excel 2024, follow these steps:

1. **Select the Data**: Highlight the cells you want to format. This can be a column, a row, several cells, or an entire spreadsheet, depending on what part of your data needs to be visually analyzed.

2. **Choose a Formatting Rule**: Navigate to the **Home** tab on the Ribbon and click on **Conditional Formatting**. Here, you'll find a variety of rules to apply:
   - **Highlight Cell Rules**: Color cells based on specific conditions, such as cells that are greater than a certain value, less than a value, between two values, or equal to a certain figure.
   - **Top/Bottom Rules**: Highlight only the top or bottom ranked values, such as the top 10 items or the bottom 10%.
   - **Data Bars or Color Scales**: Apply a color gradient. Data bars fill part of the cells with a color bar, proportional to the cell's value in the selected range.
   - **Icon Sets**: Apply icons to cells based on their value relative to other cells in the selected range, such as directional arrows, shapes, or indicators that show increasing or decreasing values.

3. **Customize the Rule**: After selecting a rule, customize it by specifying the criteria. For example, if you're using a 'Greater Than' rule, you'll need to define what value must be exceeded for the formatting to apply.

Practical Applications of Conditional Formatting

Imagine you are analyzing sales data to identify which products are performing above or below expectations:

- **Heat Maps**: Use color scales to create a heat map of sales performance across different regions. Higher sales numbers could be colored in warm colors like red and orange, while lower sales appear in cooler colors like blue and green.
- **Data Bars**: Add data bars to monthly sales figures to give a quick visual representation of how each month's sales stack up against others.
- **Icon Sets**: Use icons to indicate whether sales targets are being met, exceeded, or not achieved. An upward green arrow could show where targets are exceeded, a sideways yellow arrow where targets are met, and a downward red arrow where they are not.

Advantages of Using Conditional Formatting

Conditional formatting transforms the way data is consumed by making it digestible at a glance:

- **Immediate Data Insights**: Visual patterns are easier to recognize than raw numbers, enabling faster analysis and decision-making.
- **Dynamic Data Interaction**: As data changes over time, the conditional formatting rules dynamically adjust, providing real-time visual feedback.
- **Error Detection**: Highlighting outliers or incorrect entries quickly to clean data sets, ensuring the accuracy of your analysis.

Best Practices for Conditional Formatting

To maximize the effectiveness of conditional formatting, consider the following:

- **Avoid Over-formatting**: Too much conditional formatting can make a spreadsheet difficult to read. Use it sparingly to highlight the most crucial information.
- **Keep Color Blindness in Mind**: Choose color schemes that are accessible to those with color vision deficiencies. Tools like color blind palettes ensure that your formatting is helpful to all users.
- **Document Your Rules**: Maintain documentation of the rules applied, especially in complex sheets. This practice helps in maintaining or updating the sheet in the future.

Conditional formatting in Excel 2024 is more than just an aesthetic tool; it is a critical component of effective data analysis. By enabling you to quickly discern which numbers are most relevant, which trends are emerging, and where your attention is needed most, conditional formatting helps turn raw data into actionable insights, driving smarter business decisions.

Whether you're a seasoned data analyst or a novice to Excel, mastering this feature will enhance your ability to understand and utilize your data fully.

INTRODUCTION TO PIVOTTABLES

In the realm of Excel 2024, one of the most powerful tools at your disposal for dissecting and understanding large datasets is the PivotTable. This feature acts like a data prism, bending and refracting your data into various light—into summaries and aggregations that reveal patterns and insights which might otherwise remain obscured in the raw data mass.

The Fundamentals of PivotTables

A PivotTable is essentially a data summarization tool that lets you reorganize, sort, group, and summarize your data. It allows for examining the data from different perspectives and making comparisons. Imagine you are the captain of a vessel in the vast ocean of your data. A PivotTable gives you the navigation tools to steer and anchor your data exactly where you need it, providing a detailed map of your numbers.

Creating Your First PivotTable

Creating a PivotTable in Excel 2024 can be approached as an exciting journey into the heart of your data:

1. **Select Your Data**: PivotTables work best with well-organized data. Ideally, your data should be in a list format, with distinct columns containing related data, each column bearing a clear header.
2. **Insert a PivotTable**:
   - Navigate to the **Insert** tab and select **PivotTable**.
   - Excel will automatically suggest the data range to analyze if you've selected your dataset before clicking **PivotTable**.
   - Decide whether the PivotTable will be placed in a new worksheet or an existing one, depending on how you want to view the summarized data alongside your raw data.
3. **Define the PivotTable Structure**:
   - Once your PivotTable is created, you'll drag fields into one of the four areas in the PivotTable Field List: **Filters**, **Columns**, **Rows**, and **Values**.
   - The **Rows** and **Columns** will define what headings appear around the table. These could be dates, product names, regions, etc.

- The **Values** area is where you decide how to summarize the data—whether you're summing numbers, averaging them, or counting data entries.
- The **Filters** area allows you to include only certain elements in the report, like filtering to show data for a specific year or product.

Practical Applications of PivotTables

Consider you're a sales manager looking to analyze annual sales data:

- **Data Segmentation**: Use a PivotTable to break down sales by product and region. Drag product names to the rows, region names to the columns, and sales totals to the values area.
- **Time Analysis**: Drag date fields to the columns to see how sales trends develop over time.
- **Comparative Analysis**: Use filters to compare performance across different sales teams or between different time periods.

Deepening Insights with PivotTables

PivotTables can be enhanced with further functionalities to deepen your analysis:

- **Calculated Fields**: Add your formulas within a PivotTable to create custom calculations that don't exist in your source data, like calculating the profit margin on each item sold.
- **Grouping Data**: Group data in a PivotTable to see higher-level summaries. For example, group date fields into months and years to see broader trends.
- **Slicers**: These are visual filters. Adding slicers to your PivotTable makes it easier to filter the data interactively, perfect for presentations or when working with dynamic datasets.

Best Practices for PivotTables

To leverage the full power of PivotTables effectively:

- **Keep Source Data Clean**: Ensure your data is free of blank rows and columns, and that each column has a header.
- **Regularly Refresh**: If your data source is updated, refresh your PivotTable to reflect these changes by right-clicking within the table and selecting **Refresh**.
- **Design With the End in Mind**: Before you build your PivotTable, consider what insights you need to extract. This foresight will guide how you set up your rows, columns, filters, and values.

PivotTables in Excel 2024 offer a dynamic way to interact with your data. By transforming extensive and complex raw data into manageable summaries, PivotTables provide a powerful means of analysis that aids in making informed, data-driven decisions. With these tools, you transform from a passive observer of your data to an active explorer, uncovering the rich insights that lie within your data's depths.

6. CHARTS AND GRAPHS

SELECTING THE RIGHT CHART TYPE

In the world of data visualization, selecting the right chart type is akin to choosing the correct lens through which to view a story. Each chart type has a unique way of illuminating your data, revealing different insights and guiding the observer toward understanding complex information swiftly and intuitively. Excel 2024 offers a vast array of chart types designed to cater to diverse analytical needs, ensuring that for every type of data, there is an optimal way to visualize it.

Understanding Chart Types and Their Uses

When it comes to Excel, the art of choosing the right chart type involves matching the graphical representation with the specific narrative you wish to tell with your data. Here's how to navigate this selection process effectively:

Column and Bar Charts

Column charts are ideal for showing changes over time or comparing differences between items. Categories are typically organized along the horizontal axis and values along the vertical axis. They are best used when category labels are text, and you have fewer than 10 items to compare.

Bar charts work similarly to column charts but are particularly effective when you have long category names or when there are many categories. By displaying categories horizontally, bar charts make the labels easier to read.

Line Charts

Line charts are perfect for displaying trends over time (years, months, or days) or continuous data sequences. When dealing with many data points and the order is necessary to the viewer, a line chart is often the best choice. It is particularly effective in showing how a variable changes in response to another variable, such as time.

Pie and Doughnut Charts

Pie charts are used to show percentages or proportional data as part of a whole. They are most effective when you want to highlight significant segments within your data and when your dataset contains fewer than five categories to compare. Each slice of the pie shows the size of a category in a straightforward, visual manner.

Doughnut charts serve a similar purpose but can contain more than one series of data, offering a more detailed breakdown of the proportions.

Scatter Plots and Bubble Charts

Scatter plots are used for displaying and observing relationships between two numerical variables. Each data point represents the intersection of data on the horizontal and vertical axes. Scatter plots are especially useful for determining if two variables are correlated or if they follow a certain trend pattern.

Bubble charts are a variation of scatter plots where each data point also has a size dimension, allowing you to incorporate a third data variable into the visualization.

Area Charts

Area charts are essentially line charts but with the space below the line filled with color. They are useful for demonstrating the magnitude of change over time and can be used to show the contribution of multiple parts to a whole, especially when the total across time is as important as the individual contributions.

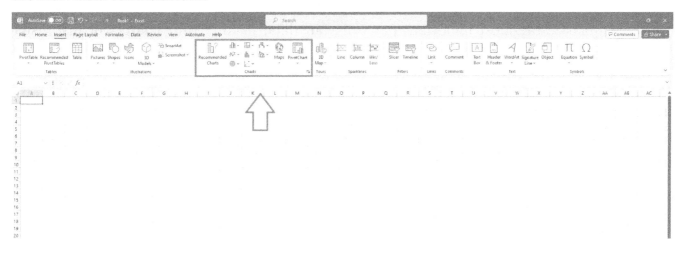

Best Practices for Selecting Chart Types

To ensure that your chosen chart type effectively communicates the intended message of your data, consider the following guidelines:

- **Know Your Audience**: Understand the level of detail and complexity your audience can comfortably handle.
- **Define Your Objective**: Clearly define what you want your audience to take away from the chart. Are you trying to show a trend, a relationship, or a composition?
- **Keep It Simple**: Opt for the simplest chart type that can effectively communicate your data. Overly complex charts can confuse and distract from the key message.

- **Use Color Wisely**: Use color to highlight important data points or trends and to guide the viewer's attention through the data.
- **Label Clearly**: Make sure all parts of your chart are clearly labeled—axes, series, and legends. Labels are crucial for understanding the chart without additional explanations.

Choosing the right chart type in Excel 2024 is an essential skill in data visualization, playing a pivotal role in how effectively data-driven insights are communicated. Each chart type serves a specific purpose and, when matched correctly with the data at hand, can transform raw data into compelling stories.

By mastering the use of various chart types, you enhance your ability to present data in ways that are not only visually appealing but also maximally informative, making complex data accessible and understandable for all.

CUSTOMIZING CHARTS

Customizing charts in Excel 2024 is akin to painting a picture that needs to tell a story at a glance. The raw data provides the outline, but how you color it in—the styles, colors, and elements you choose—can significantly enhance its impact and readability. This process of customization allows you to emphasize the most important parts of your data, making your charts not just visual representations but powerful narratives that speak directly to your audience.

The Art of Chart Customization

When you create a chart in Excel, it often requires adjustments to perfectly suit your presentation or report's needs. Customizing a chart can involve modifying its layout, style, colors, and adding elements like titles or labels. Each of these aspects plays a critical role in making your chart clear and engaging.

Chart Styles and Layouts

Excel 2024 offers a range of predefined chart styles and layouts that can be applied with just a few clicks. These are designed to change the overall appearance of your chart, including colors and effects. To apply a different style:

1. Select your chart to activate the Chart Tools on the ribbon.
2. Click on the **Design** tab.
3. Browse the chart styles in the **Chart Styles** group to preview and select a new style.

While these predefined styles provide a quick and easy way to enhance the visual appeal of your charts, they may not always fit your specific needs or the branding guidelines of your organization.

Customizing Chart Elements

To further refine your chart, you might want to adjust individual elements. This could involve adding, removing, or altering:

- **Chart Titles and Axis Titles**: Provide context to what the chart represents. You can customize the text, font, size, and color to make them stand out or blend with your design.
- **Legend**: Modify its position or format it to make the chart easier to understand, especially if you're working with multiple data series.
- **Data Labels**: These can be crucial for directly showing key numbers in the chart. Position, format, and even the content of data labels can be customized—for instance, showing percentage rather than value in a pie chart.
- **Axes**: Adjusting the scale of axes can help highlight particular aspects of your data. You might also want to change the way labels are formatted or positioned.

Color Customization

Colors play a pivotal role in chart readability and aesthetics. Choosing the right color palette can enhance data visualization by providing contrast and focus where needed.

1. Click on the element you wish to recolor—this could be the plot area, data series, or background.
2. Right-click and select **Format**.
3. Choose from the color options, or select **More Colors** for custom shades. This is particularly useful for adhering to corporate branding or making your chart accessible to those with color vision deficiencies.

Adding Rich Media Elements

Excel 2024 allows the integration of rich media elements into charts:

- **Images**: You can insert images into chart backgrounds or plot areas to add visual interest or clarify the data context.
- **Shapes and Annotations**: Adding arrows, lines, or shapes can help highlight important trends or data points. Annotations can be used to draw attention to specific details or provide additional information.

Best Practices for Chart Customization

- **Consistency is Key**: Ensure that your charts maintain a consistent style within a document or across a series of presentations. This helps in reinforcing brand identity and improving the professional quality of your output.

- **Simplicity Over Complexity**: While it's tempting to use elaborate designs and effects, simplicity often enhances understanding. Avoid cluttering your chart with too many elements that might distract from the key message.

- **Test for Readability**: Always preview your charts on different devices and in different formats (if your report is to be printed or displayed online). This testing ensures that your charts communicate effectively across all intended mediums.

Customizing charts in Excel 2024 is not just about making your data 'pretty'; it's about strategic enhancement to tell your data's story more effectively. Whether it's a presentation for stakeholders, an annual report, or an academic paper, the way you customize your charts can significantly impact how your audience interprets the data, making your findings not only seen but understood.

DYNAMIC CHART TECHNIQUES

In the evolving landscape of Excel 2024, dynamic chart techniques stand at the forefront of data visualization, offering tools not just to display static images but to create visuals that adapt, change, and interact based on your data's behavior or user input. These techniques extend the utility of traditional charts, transforming them into living elements of your data analysis efforts. They are akin to digital chameleons, adjusting their colors and patterns to the environment—your data environment, that is.

The Essence of Dynamic Charts

Dynamic charts in Excel 2024 are not just visually appealing; they are functional, flexible, and responsive. They are designed to automatically update as the underlying data changes, providing a real-time view of trends and metrics that are crucial for rapid decision-making processes. This dynamic capability ensures that your visual representations are always current, eliminating the need for manual updates every time the data changes.

Creating a Dynamic Chart

To build a dynamic chart, you begin with a solid foundation—well-structured data and a basic understanding of chart creation. Then, you enhance this setup with elements that allow the chart to respond to data changes or user interactions.

1. Setting Up the Data

Ensure your data is in a format conducive to dynamic updating. This might involve organizing data into tables, which Excel can easily monitor for changes and adjustments.

2. Using Excel Tables

Convert your data range into an Excel table by selecting the range and using the **Insert > Table** option. Tables in Excel are inherently dynamic; they automatically expand to include new data added to adjacent rows or columns, and any charts derived from table data will update accordingly.

3. Defining Dynamic Named Ranges

Named ranges can also be made dynamic by using Excel formulas. For instance, if your data will expand over time, you can use a formula like:

```
=OFFSET(Sheet1!$A$1,0,0,COUNTA(Sheet1!$A:$A),1)
```

This formula creates a range that starts at A1 and expands downward as new entries are added to column A.

4. Applying Dynamic Ranges to Charts

Once you have defined a dynamic named range, use this range as the source for your chart. Any chart created with this range will automatically update when new data is added to the range.

Advanced Dynamic Techniques

To further enhance the responsiveness of your charts, consider integrating form controls like sliders, dropdown lists, or checkboxes that let users interact with the data visualized in the chart.

5. Inserting Form Controls

Add form controls from the **Developer** tab, under **Insert**. For example, a combo box can allow users to select different data series to display in a chart.

6. Linking Controls to Chart Data

Link form controls to your chart data by using cell links and simple VBA scripts or Excel functions. For example, you might set up a combo box that lets users select a year, and the chart displays data corresponding to that year.

Use Cases for Dynamic Charts

- **Financial Dashboards**: Dynamic charts are ideal for financial dashboards where key performance indicators (KPIs) need to be monitored continuously, such as monthly sales growth, year-to-date expenses, or profitability trends.
- **Project Management**: Use dynamic Gantt charts to track project timelines and milestones. As project data is updated, the Gantt chart reflects changes in real-time, helping project managers adjust timelines and resources efficiently.
- **Market Analysis**: In market analysis, dynamic charts can help track stock prices or market trends. Analysts can adjust the range of data viewed based on a selected time frame, providing deeper insights into market movements.

Best Practices for Dynamic Charts

- **Simplicity is Key**: While dynamic charts offer advanced capabilities, keeping them simple and focused on specific insights can enhance their effectiveness.
- **Test Thoroughly**: Dynamic charts should be tested extensively to ensure they perform as expected as data changes. This includes testing under different scenarios to simulate how users might interact with the chart.
- **Document Functionality**: Ensure that the functionality of any dynamic elements is well-documented, especially if the spreadsheet will be used by others. This documentation should include instructions on how to update data and how to use any interactive controls.

Dynamic chart techniques in Excel 2024 transform traditional charts from static snapshots of data into vibrant, interactive visual tools that offer real-time insights. As you harness these dynamic capabilities, you empower your charts to tell more compelling, timely, and interactive data stories, making them not just informative but also engaging.

7. UTILIZING EXCEL FUNCTIONS

LOGICAL FUNCTIONS

In the expansive toolkit of Excel 2024, logical functions stand out as essential instruments for decision-making and data analysis, enabling users to perform complex checks and balances within their datasets. These functions are the very sinews that connect data conditions to actionable insights, allowing for dynamic responses based on specific criteria defined within your spreadsheet.

Understanding Logical Functions

Logical functions in Excel evaluate conditions you specify and respond with a result that can be either TRUE or FALSE. These functions are particularly powerful when combined with other features of Excel to automate processes, enable smart decision trees, and manage large sets of data efficiently by filtering through and responding to specific criteria.

The Core Logical Functions

1. **IF Function**: The bread and butter of logical operations in Excel. The **IF** function checks whether a condition is met, and returns one value if TRUE, and another if FALSE.

```
=IF(condition, value_if_true, value_if_false)
```

For example, **=IF(A1 > 10, "High", "Low")** checks if the value in A1 is greater than 10 and returns **High** if true, or **Low** if false.

2. **AND & OR Functions**: These are used to test multiple conditions at once. **AND** returns TRUE if all conditions are true. **OR** returns TRUE if any of the conditions are true.

```
=AND(condition1, condition2, ...)
=OR(condition1, condition2, ...)
```

For instance, **=AND(A1 > 10, A1 < 20)** will only return TRUE if A1 is greater than 10 AND less than 20.

3. **NOT Function**: This function reverses the logic of its argument: if given TRUE, it returns FALSE; if given FALSE, it returns TRUE.

```
=NOT(condition)
```

An example could be **=NOT(A1 > 10)**, which will be TRUE if A1 is not greater than 10.

4. **IFERROR Function**: This function returns a custom result if an error is found in the formula, otherwise it returns the formula result.

```
=IFERROR(value, value_if_error)
```

For example, **=IFERROR(1/0, "Error in calculation")** would return "Error in calculation" because dividing by zero is an error.

5. **IFS Function** (available in newer versions of Excel): Used for cases where you need to evaluate multiple conditions.

```
=IFS(condition1, value1, condition2, value2, ...)
```

This function checks conditions in the order they are given and returns the value for the first TRUE condition.

Practical Applications of Logical Functions

Logical functions are versatile tools that can be used in a myriad of practical scenarios in business analysis, project management, finance, and more:

- **Financial Reporting**: Use **IF** statements to categorize expenditures as either within budget or over budget.
- **Employee Management**: Combine **AND**, **OR**, and **IF** to evaluate employee performance based on multiple criteria such as sales targets, customer feedback, and attendance.
- **Inventory Control**: Utilize **IFERROR** along with lookup functions to manage inventory levels, providing alerts when items need restocking or when data errors occur.

Best Practices for Using Logical Functions

To effectively use logical functions in Excel 2024:

- **Clearly Define Logic**: Before implementing any function, clearly outline what you need to evaluate and how each piece of your logic connects. This clarity will help prevent errors in your logic and make maintenance easier.

- **Keep Formulas Readable**: Logical functions can quickly become complex. To keep them manageable, use named ranges to replace cell addresses, and consider breaking down very complex formulas into several simpler steps.
- **Use Helper Columns**: For complex logical tests, use helper columns to compute intermediate results. This approach makes your final formula simpler and your spreadsheet easier to audit and understand.
- **Test Extensively**: Given the binary nature of logical functions, small mistakes can lead to incorrect conclusions. Test your formulas thoroughly to ensure they behave as expected under all relevant scenarios.

Logical functions in Excel allow you to make your spreadsheets think and respond intelligently to the data they contain. Mastering these functions enables you to build more dynamic, responsive, and robust Excel models, turning static data into a dynamic toolkit capable of providing deeper insights and supporting smarter business decisions.

TEXT MANIPULATION FUNCTIONS

Mastering text manipulation functions in Excel 2024 is akin to being a wordsmith in the world of data, where textual content must be shaped, refined, and polished to meet the needs of rigorous data processing and presentation. Text functions allow you to extract, combine, convert, and analyze strings of text within your datasets, turning raw textual data into structured, useful information that can be easily understood and analyzed.

The Importance of Text Functions in Excel

Excel is not only a powerful tool for numerical calculations but also for managing and manipulating text. Whether it's formatting names, addresses, or extracting specific information from a string of text, Excel's text manipulation functions handle these tasks efficiently. These functions become indispensable when preparing data for reports, ensuring data integrity, or even when cleaning up imported data.

Key Text Manipulation Functions

To harness the full potential of Excel's text manipulation capabilities, one must understand several key functions:

CONCATENATE and CONCAT

These functions are used to combine two or more text strings into one. **CONCATENATE** has been a staple in Excel but is now succeeded by **CONCAT**, which is more flexible and powerful.

- **Syntax**: **=CONCAT(text1, [text2], …)**
- **Example**: **=CONCAT("Data", " Analysis")** results in "Data Analysis".

LEFT, MID, and RIGHT

These functions extract substrings from a piece of text based on the number of characters specified, from the start, middle, or end of the text, respectively.

- **LEFT Syntax**: **=LEFT(text, number_of_characters)**
- **MID Syntax**: **=MID(text, start_position, number_of_characters)**
- **RIGHT Syntax**: **=RIGHT(text, number_of_characters)**
- **Example**: **=LEFT("Excel 2024", 5)** returns "Excel".

LOWER, UPPER, and PROPER

These functions convert text to lower case, upper case, or proper case (where the first letter of each word is capitalized), respectively.

- **Syntax**: **=LOWER(text)**, **=UPPER(text)**, **=PROPER(text)**
- **Example**: **=UPPER("excel")** results in "EXCEL".

TRIM

This function removes extra spaces from text except for single spaces between words, which is particularly useful when cleaning data imported from other systems or formats.

- **Syntax**: **=TRIM(text)**
- **Example**: **=TRIM(" Excel 2024 ")** results in "Excel 2024".

SEARCH and FIND

These functions are used to locate the position of one text string within another, useful for extracting or manipulating specific data. **SEARCH** is case-insensitive, whereas **FIND** is case-sensitive.

- **SEARCH Syntax**: **=SEARCH(find_text, within_text, [start_num])**
- **FIND Syntax**: **=FIND(find_text, within_text, [start_num])**
- **Example**: **=SEARCH("2024", "Excel 2024")** returns 7.

Practical Applications of Text Functions

Excel's text functions can be applied in various practical scenarios:

- **Data Cleaning**: Use **TRIM**, **LOWER**, and **PROPER** to clean up and standardize text data, such as names and addresses.
- **Data Extraction**: Use **LEFT**, **MID**, and **RIGHT** to extract specific information from a structured text string, such as extracting area codes from phone numbers.
- **Dynamic Data Combination**: Use **CONCAT** to dynamically combine data from different cells into a formatted text string, useful in creating emails, messages, or reports.

Best Practices for Using Text Functions

When employing text functions in Excel 2024:

- **Combine Functions for Powerful Formulas**: Many text tasks require combining several functions. For example, to extract the first name from a full name where names are separated by a space, you might use **=LEFT(A1, SEARCH(" ", A1)-1)**.
- **Use Array Formulas for Bulk Processing**: When you need to apply a text function to a range of cells, consider using array formulas to handle multiple values simultaneously.
- **Test Edge Cases**: Text data often includes anomalies. Test your formulas with various edge cases to ensure they handle all possible text scenarios.

By integrating these text manipulation functions into your Excel workflow, you transform plain data into structured information that enhances clarity and increases the analytical value of your datasets. These tools not only save time but also bolster the reliability of your data-driven insights, proving essential in any scenario where data needs to be reported, analyzed, or presented.

DATE AND TIME FUNCTIONS

Mastering date and time functions in Excel 2024 is like unlocking a new dimension of data analysis, allowing you to delve into temporal patterns, sequences, and durations that are critical for any comprehensive analysis. These functions handle everything from simple date and time calculations to complex scheduling and tracking. Understanding how to use these tools effectively can transform raw date and time data into insightful, actionable information.

The Significance of Date and Time Functions

Date and time data is ubiquitous in almost every field, whether you are analyzing sales trends, managing project timelines, scheduling posts, or tracking historical records. Excel's date and time functions help you extract more detailed insights from this data, perform time-based calculations, and organize your data more efficiently.

Core Date and Time Functions in Excel 2024

Excel 2024 offers a robust set of functions designed to handle various aspects of date and time calculations:

NOW and TODAY

- **NOW()**: Returns the current date and time every time the worksheet recalculates.
- **TODAY()**: Provides the current date but does not include time.

These functions are particularly useful for dynamic reporting and for calculations that depend on the current date or time.

DATE, TIME, and DATEVALUE, TIMEVALUE

- **DATE(year, month, day)**: Creates a date value for the dates constructed from the year, month, and day arguments.
- **TIME(hour, minute, second)**: Generates a time value from hour, minute, and second components.
- **DATEVALUE("date_text")**: Converts a date in the form of text to a serial number that Excel recognizes as a date.
- **TIMEVALUE("time_text")**: Turns a time represented as text into a serial number Excel recognizes as a time.

These functions allow for the creation and manipulation of date and time values, essential for tasks that involve the construction or parsing of dates and times from raw data.

EDATE and EOMONTH

- **EDATE(start_date, months)**: Calculates the date that is a specified number of months before or after a start date.
- **EOMONTH(start_date, months)**: Returns the last day of the month a specified number of months before or after the start date.

These functions are useful for financial calculations and for managing deadlines and other date-related calculations.

NETWORKDAYS and WORKDAY

- **NETWORKDAYS(start_date, end_date, [holidays])**: Returns the number of whole working days between two dates.
- **WORKDAY(start_date, days, [holidays])**: Calculates a date a certain number of working days before or after a date.

These are invaluable for project planning and for calculating working days when scheduling tasks.

Practical Applications of Date and Time Functions

Let's explore some practical scenarios where these functions can be directly applied:

- **Project Management**: Use **WORKDAY** and **NETWORKDAYS** to track project deadlines and ensure that timelines consider only business days, excluding weekends and holidays.
- **Financial Reports**: Calculate fiscal quarters or maturity dates for financial products with **EDATE** and **EOMONTH**.
- **Event Planning**: Determine the number of days until an event, or calculate follow-up dates using **DATE** and **TIME** functions.
- **Historical Data Analysis**: Convert textual date and time representations into serial numbers with **DATEVALUE** and **TIMEVALUE** for time series analysis.

Best Practices for Using Date and Time Functions

To maximize efficiency and accuracy when using date and time functions in Excel:

- **Always specify full date and time**: When entering dates or times, use the full specification to avoid ambiguities. For example, use **YEAR**, **MONTH**, and **DAY** together when using the **DATE** function.
- **Utilize dynamic formulas**: Leverage functions like **TODAY** and **NOW** for creating dynamic models that automatically update based on the current date and time.
- **Be cautious with locale settings**: Date formats can vary by locale; ensure that your Excel settings match the date formats you are entering to avoid errors.

Date and time functions in Excel 2024 empower users to handle temporal data with precision and ease. By integrating these functions into your spreadsheets, you enhance your ability to analyze trends over time, forecast future dates, and manage schedules effectively, all while ensuring your data remains as dynamic and responsive as the world around it.

8. ADVANCED FORMULAS

NESTED FUNCTIONS

In the complex world of data analysis within Excel 2024, nested functions are akin to multi-layered strategies in a chess game, where each move is calculated to build upon the previous one, creating a sophisticated plan that anticipates various outcomes and counters potential obstacles. This level of formula construction allows you to combine multiple functions into a single formula, enabling detailed and condition-specific analyses that can handle diverse and dynamic datasets effectively.

What Are Nested Functions?

Nested functions in Excel involve placing one function inside another as part of the argument. This technique allows you to achieve complex data manipulations within a single cell, reducing the need for multiple columns of intermediate results and thus streamlining your data processing workflows.

The Architecture of Nested Functions

Imagine constructing a building where each floor's design depends intricately on the one below it. Similarly, each function in a nested formula must be correctly positioned and logically ordered for the entire expression to work correctly. The outer function forms the facade, encapsulating and modifying the result of the inner function(s).

Constructing a Nested Function

To build a nested function, start with identifying the core outcome you need. This outcome determines which functions you'll combine. For example, if you need to extract a piece of text based on a numerical condition, you might nest **IF** inside **LEFT** or **MID**.

1. **Identify the core function**: This is the function that will ultimately deliver your needed outcome.
2. **Determine supporting functions**: These are the functions that prepare, filter, or modify the data to be used by the core function.
3. **Layer your functions**: Begin by writing the innermost function, and progressively wrap it with the outer functions.

Example of Nested Functions

Suppose you need to categorize expenditures based on amount, where you also need to extract the department code from a description field only if the expenditure is above a certain threshold:

```
=IF(A1 > 1000, LEFT(B1, 3), "N/A")
```

In this formula:

- **LEFT(B1, 3)** is the inner function, extracting the first three characters from the description in **B1**.
- **IF(A1 > 1000, ..., "N/A")** is the outer function, deciding whether to show the department code or "N/A" based on the amount in **A1**.

Practical Applications

Nested functions are incredibly useful in scenarios where data conditions are layered:

- **Financial Analysis**: Calculate conditional bonuses or taxes where multiple criteria might affect the outcome.
- **Inventory Management**: Determine restocking levels based on multiple conditions like sales velocity, seasonal adjustments, and supplier reliability.
- **HR Operations**: Automate complex calculations of employee benefits or leave balances that depend on multiple factors such as tenure, job grade, and local regulations.

Best Practices for Nested Functions

To effectively use nested functions in Excel 2024, consider the following:

- **Limit Nesting Levels**: While Excel 2024 can handle numerous nesting levels, try to limit yourself to three or four to maintain readability and manageability.
- **Use Helper Columns**: When formulas get too complex, consider using helper columns to break down the formula into more manageable parts.
- **Document Your Formulas**: Always provide comments or documentation for complex nested formulas. This practice is crucial for maintenance, especially in collaborative environments.

Debugging Nested Functions

Debugging nested functions can be challenging due to their complexity:

- **Evaluate Formula Tool**: Use Excel's Evaluate Formula dialog (Formulas tab > Evaluate Formula) to step through each part of the nested formula. This tool helps you see the calculation at each step.

- **Simplify Temporarily**: Break down the nested formula into its components in separate cells to isolate errors more easily.

Nested functions, when mastered, turn your spreadsheets into powerful tools capable of handling complex logic and providing nuanced insights into your data. They allow for deeper analysis with fewer formulas, making your Excel environment cleaner and your workflows more efficient. In mastering nested functions, you equip yourself with the ability to tackle advanced data challenges, making Excel not just a tool for data entry but a powerful engine for data intelligence.

ERROR CHECKING

In the vast and intricate world of Excel 2024, where data flows as abundantly as water in a river, the potential for errors in your spreadsheet calculations can turn a smooth stream into a turbulent cascade. To harness this flow and prevent it from leading astray, robust error-checking mechanisms are essential. These tools not only identify where and why errors occur but also provide insights on how to correct them, ensuring that your data analyses remain accurate and reliable.

The Importance of Error Checking in Excel

Excel 2024 is equipped to handle complex calculations and data manipulations across countless cells. With this complexity, however, comes the increased likelihood of errors which can propagate unnoticed, leading to incorrect conclusions and decisions. Effective error checking is crucial in maintaining the integrity of your data, much like a lighthouse guiding ships safely to shore, ensuring that all numbers are correctly calculated and logically presented.

Common Types of Errors in Excel

Understanding the types of errors you might encounter in Excel can help you diagnose problems more efficiently:

- **#DIV/0!**: This error appears when a number is divided by zero.
- **#N/A**: Indicates that a value is not available to a function or formula.
- **#NAME?**: Occurs if Excel does not recognize text in a formula.

- **#NULL!**: Means you specified an intersection of two areas that do not intersect.
- **#NUM!**: Indicates that a formula has invalid numeric values.
- **#REF!**: Appears when a cell reference is not valid.
- **#VALUE!**: Occurs when the wrong type of argument or operand is used.

Strategies for Effective Error Checking

Navigating through errors requires a systematic approach to uncover and address each issue methodically:

1. Use Excel's Built-In Error Checking

Excel's built-in error checking tool automatically scans for errors and offers suggestions for correction:

- Navigate to the **Formulas** tab and click on **Error Checking**.
- This tool will guide you through each error found in the worksheet, providing explanations and possible solutions.

2. Trace Error Origins

Understanding where an error starts is crucial in resolving it:

- Use **Trace Precedents** or **Trace Dependents** features found under the **Formulas** tab. These tools draw arrows to and from the formula cell, showing which cells affect or are affected by the current cell.
- This tracing is invaluable for unraveling complex formulas where multiple cells contribute to the final result.

3. Evaluate Formulas

Breaking down formulas into their constituent parts can help isolate errors:

- The **Evaluate Formula** function, also found under the **Formulas** tab, allows you to see the calculation step-by-step. This feature is especially useful for understanding how Excel interprets your formula and where it might be going wrong.

4. Use Conditional Formatting to Identify Errors

Highlight potential errors visually using conditional formatting:

- Set up rules to highlight unusual or impossible values, such as negative totals in a series of supposed positive numbers.
- Apply conditional formats that highlight cells containing Excel's error types like **#N/A** or **#REF!**.

5. Create Error Handling in Formulas

Incorporate error handling directly in your formulas to manage known error conditions gracefully:

- Use **IFERROR** or **IFNA** to specify a return value when your formula results in an error, which can be particularly useful in keeping your data presentation clean and uncluttered.

Best Practices for Minimizing Errors

To further safeguard your spreadsheets against errors, adhere to these best practices:

- **Simplify Formulas**: Where possible, break complex formulas into smaller, manageable segments. Use helper columns if necessary to make each step clear and verifiable.
- **Consistently Review and Test**: Regularly review your formulas and calculations by cross-verifying totals and using sample data to test different scenarios.
- **Document Your Work**: Keep detailed notes on your formulas' intended behavior and any assumptions they rely on. This documentation is crucial not only for error checking but also for future reference or if another person needs to understand your work.

Error checking in Excel 2024 is not just a defensive measure; it is an integral part of a proactive strategy to ensure data accuracy and reliability. By mastering these error-checking techniques, you ensure that your analyses stand on solid ground, your decisions are well-informed, and your reports maintain the highest level of professional integrity.

ARRAY FORMULAS

Array formulas in Excel 2024 stand as a powerful emblem of the software's capacity for deep, intricate data analysis and manipulation. These formulas aren't just functions; they're finely tuned orchestras where each cell plays a part in a larger symphony of numbers, performing calculations across multiple values simultaneously. Understanding how to effectively use array formulas elevates your Excel skills from proficient to expert, allowing you to handle bulk data operations with precision and efficiency.

Understanding Array Formulas

Array formulas can perform multiple calculations on one or more items within an array, then return either a single result or multiple results. They are particularly effective for complex computations where the task involves conditional calculations across a range of cells. Imagine you're analyzing data spread across hundreds of cells. Instead of writing a separate formula for each cell, an array formula lets you gracefully execute these operations in one fell swoop.

How to Create Array Formulas

Creating an array formula in Excel involves a combination of traditional formula inputs and special keystrokes to signify to Excel that you're creating an array:

1. **Input the formula**: Start by typing your formula into the formula bar as you would any other formula.

2. **Convert to an array formula**: Instead of pressing Enter, you'll finalize the formula by pressing **Ctrl+Shift+Enter**. Excel recognizes this as an array formula and surrounds it with curly braces **{}**. This cannot be typed in manually; Excel adds them when you press **Ctrl+Shift+Enter**.

Example of an Array Formula

Suppose you want to calculate the total sales of multiple products based on certain conditions. Instead of summing each row individually, you could use an array formula like:

```
=SUM(IF(A1:A100="Product X", B1:B100, 0))
```

Here, you check each cell in **A1:A100** for "Product X". If the condition is met, the corresponding cell from **B1:B100** is included in the sum. Pressing **Ctrl+Shift+Enter** turns this into an array formula that processes the entire array at once.

When to Use Array Formulas

Array formulas are incredibly versatile and can be used in a variety of scenarios, including:

- **Complex Calculations**: When you need to perform calculations that depend on multiple conditions across a dataset.
- **Data Analysis**: For summarizing or transforming data without altering the original dataset.
- **Simultaneous Calculations**: When outcomes for a range of cells depend on other arrays or ranges.

Advanced Uses of Array Formulas

Beyond basic calculations, array formulas can be used to create sophisticated data manipulations:

- **CSE Arrays**: Traditional array formulas that require Ctrl+Shift+Enter to activate.
- **Dynamic Array Functions**: With Excel 2024, formulas that return arrays automatically spill over into adjacent cells without needing special keystrokes.

Example of a Dynamic Array Formula

Imagine you have a list of sales data and you want to filter out all sales below a certain threshold:

```
=FILTER(A2:B100, B2:B100>50)
```

This dynamic array formula in Excel 2024 automatically spills the results into the cells below without needing **Ctrl+Shift+Enter**.

Best Practices for Array Formulas

- **Simplicity is key**: While array formulas are powerful, they can also become complex and difficult to debug. Where possible, keep your formulas simple or break complex problems into smaller parts.
- **Document your work**: Always comment your array formulas or provide documentation alongside them. This will help you and others understand the logic behind the formula, especially if the workbook will be shared.
- **Performance considerations**: Array formulas can slow down your workbook if used extensively on large data sets. Always test performance and seek alternatives like pivot tables or built-in functions where appropriate.

Array formulas, especially in their dynamic form in Excel 2024, represent some of the most advanced capabilities available to data analysts. By leveraging these formulas, you can enhance your productivity, increase the reliability of your data processing, and present your findings with greater sophistication and accuracy. These formulas not only compute across multiple data points but also bring depth and nuance to your data analysis, transforming numbers into narratives that drive insightful decisions.

PART III: BEYOND BASIC - ELEVATING YOUR EXCEL SKILLS

9. MASTERING EXCEL'S DATABASE FUNCTIONS

EFFECTIVE USE OF LOOKUP FUNCTIONS

In the expansive toolset of Excel 2024, LOOKUP functions are indispensable navigational aids, helping users traverse vast data landscapes to pinpoint specific information efficiently and accurately. Just as a navigator uses stars to guide a ship through the night, Excel users rely on LOOKUP functions to steer through columns of data to find the values they need.

Introduction to LOOKUP Functions

LOOKUP functions in Excel are designed to search for one item in an array or range and return a corresponding item in the same position from a second array or range. These functions are critical in data management tasks such as data reconciliation, searching records, and automating data entries.

Types of LOOKUP Functions

Excel 2024 provides several variations of LOOKUP functions, each suited to different types of data searches and organizational needs:

VLOOKUP (Vertical Lookup)

The VLOOKUP function searches for a value in the first column of a table array and returns a value in the same row from a specified column.

- **Syntax**: =VLOOKUP(lookup_value, table_array, col_index_num, [range_lookup])
- **Example**: If you need to find a person's phone number in a table where the first column contains names and the second column contains phone numbers, you would use: **=VLOOKUP("John Doe", A2:B100, 2, FALSE)**. This formula looks for "John Doe" in the first column between rows 2 and 100 and returns the value from the second column.

HLOOKUP (Horizontal Lookup)

Similar to VLOOKUP, HLOOKUP searches for a value across the top row of a table and returns a value in the same column from a row you specify.

- **Syntax**: =HLOOKUP(lookup_value, table_array, row_index_num, [range_lookup])
- **Example**: To find information in a dataset where data headers are arranged horizontally, you might use: **=HLOOKUP("Total Sales", A1:Z1, 5, FALSE)** to find "Total Sales" across the first row and return the value from the fifth row.

XLOOKUP (Extended Lookup)

Introduced in newer versions of Excel, XLOOKUP replaces both VLOOKUP and HLOOKUP by offering more flexibility and straightforward syntax.

- **Syntax**: =XLOOKUP(lookup_value, lookup_array, return_array, [if_not_found], [match_mode], [search_mode])
- **Example**: To find "John Doe's" phone number in an updated dataset: **=XLOOKUP("John Doe", A2:A100, B2:B100, "Not Found")**.

Best Practices for Using LOOKUP Functions

To maximize the effectiveness and accuracy of LOOKUP functions in Excel 2024, consider these guidelines:

- **Accurate Data Organization**: Ensure your data is well-organized and sorted, especially if your lookup function assumes sorted data (setting the range_lookup argument to TRUE in VLOOKUP, for instance).
- **Use Absolute References for Table Arrays**: When setting up your formula, make sure your table_array uses absolute references (e.g., **$A$2:$B$100**) to prevent errors if you copy or move the formula to other cells.
- **Handle Errors Gracefully**: Incorporate error-handling to manage instances where the lookup value is not found. For VLOOKUP and HLOOKUP, wrap your formula in an IFERROR function to return a custom message instead of an error code.

Advanced Scenarios

LOOKUP functions are not just for simple searches; they can be creatively used in more complex scenarios:

- **Dynamic Data Retrieval**: Combine LOOKUP functions with other functions like IF and ISERROR to create dynamic reports that adjust content based on user input or other external conditions.

- **Two-way Lookups**: Use a combination of HLOOKUP and VLOOKUP to perform a two-way lookup, which searches for a value at the intersection of a specific row and column in a data matrix.

In essence, mastering the LOOKUP functions in Excel 2024 is about enhancing your ability to navigate data efficiently and accurately. As with any navigation, the key is knowing not only your destination but understanding the best path to get there. In the vast sea of data that modern Excel users must navigate, LOOKUP functions are your compass and map, guiding you to the information you need with precision and reliability. Whether reconciling vast databases or simply fetching details from a small dataset, these functions ensure you reach your data destination effectively.

EXPLORING MATCH AND INDEX FUNCTIONS

In the intricate world of Excel 2024, the MATCH and INDEX functions stand as powerful tools, acting like navigational aids that help users locate and retrieve data from a vast sea of information. Unlike more straightforward lookup functions, MATCH and INDEX offer a flexible, robust alternative for handling complex lookups. This combination allows you to search and retrieve data dynamically, catering to sophisticated data analysis needs that go beyond basic lookup functionalities.

Understanding MATCH and INDEX

The strength of MATCH and INDEX lies in their versatility and power, providing users the ability to perform lookups that are both horizontal and vertical, and even two-dimensional searches. Here's how these functions work:

The MATCH Function

MATCH searches for a specified item in a range of cells, and then returns the position of that item within the range. It is typically used to locate the position of a particular value within a column or row.

- **Syntax**: =MATCH(lookup_value, lookup_array, [match_type])
- **Example**: If you want to find the position of a specific employee's name in a list, you might use =MATCH("John Doe", A2:A100, 0). This formula returns the position of "John Doe" within the range A2:A100.

The INDEX Function

INDEX returns the value of a cell in a specific position within a range. It is often used in conjunction with MATCH to retrieve a new value based on the position identified.

- **Syntax**: =INDEX(array, row_num, [column_num])
- **Example**: To retrieve the phone number of "John Doe" from a list where the MATCH function has found the position, you would use =INDEX(B2:B100, MATCH("John Doe", A2:A100, 0)).

Combining MATCH and INDEX

Together, MATCH and INDEX are particularly powerful. While MATCH locates the position of a data point in one array, INDEX retrieves the value at that position in another array. This partnership allows for dynamic data retrieval based on variable conditions and is highly effective for two-dimensional lookups across rows and columns.

Practical Applications

Consider a scenario in which you need to find specific information in a data table that is not organized in a manner conducive to straightforward lookups:

- **Human Resources**: Find an employee's start date by locating the row with their employee ID using MATCH and retrieving the start date from that row with INDEX.
- **Sales Data Analysis**: Retrieve sales figures from a complex dataset where sales are listed by month and product type across multiple columns and rows.
- **Inventory Management**: Track inventory levels across various products stored in different warehouse locations, with data spread over multiple sheets or tables.

Advanced Tips for Using MATCH and INDEX

- **Dynamic Ranges**: Use MATCH and INDEX to work with dynamic ranges that change size or position over time, ensuring your formulas always refer to the correct data.

- **Error Handling**: Incorporate error handling in your MATCH and INDEX formulas to manage instances where no match is found. Wrap your MATCH function within an IFERROR to return a custom error message or an alternative calculation when needed.
- **Array Formulas**: Enhance the capability of MATCH and INDEX by using them within array formulas to perform multiple lookups simultaneously.

Best Practices for MATCH and INDEX

- **Data Verification**: Always verify the accuracy of the data being retrieved, especially when dealing with large datasets where errors may not be immediately apparent.
- **Documentation**: Maintain clear documentation of how and why MATCH and INDEX are used in your workbooks. This is crucial for troubleshooting and for understanding by other users or future audits.
- **Performance Considerations**: Be mindful of performance when using these functions extensively in large workbooks. Array formulas, in particular, can slow down performance if overused.

The MATCH and INDEX functions in Excel 2024 serve as a testament to the software's depth and flexibility, providing users with sophisticated tools to navigate and manipulate large datasets efficiently. By mastering these functions, you unlock advanced capabilities in data retrieval and analysis, ensuring that your work in Excel is not only productive but also robust and adaptable to complex, dynamic data environments. Whether you're managing payroll databases, analyzing annual financial reports, or maintaining inventory records, MATCH and INDEX help you achieve greater precision and efficiency in your data handling tasks.

ADVANCED DATABASE TECHNIQUES

In the sophisticated realm of Excel 2024, advanced database techniques empower users to handle, analyze, and manipulate large datasets with unprecedented precision and efficiency. These techniques extend beyond basic functions, offering tools that can significantly elevate one's capacity to perform complex analyses and provide deeper insights into the underlying data. These are not just functionalities; they are the keystones in the arch of data management that turn raw data into strategic assets.

Understanding Advanced Database Techniques

At the heart of Excel's power is its ability to act almost like a relational database, managing extensive datasets with functions that can query, summarize, transform, and extract data based on specific criteria. This capability is crucial for users who deal with large volumes of data across various fields such as finance, marketing, human resources, and more.

Key Techniques for Mastering Excel's Database Functions

Using Advanced Filter to Extract Data

Excel's Advanced Filter feature goes beyond simple filtering to allow for complex criteria across multiple columns. It supports the use of logical operators like AND and OR within the filtering process, enabling the extraction of records that meet highly specific conditions.

- **Setup**: Define your criteria range on the sheet, specifying the conditions under which data should be extracted.
- **Execution**: Select the Advanced Filter under the Data tab and specify the list range, criteria range, and whether you want to filter the data in place or to another location.

Database Functions

Excel includes a suite of functions designed specifically for managing databases, each function prefixed with "D-" (such as **DSUM**, **DAVERAGE**, **DCOUNT**). These functions are powerful tools for performing calculations on data that meets specific conditions.

- **Example**: **=DSUM(database, field, criteria)** calculates the sum of values in a field in the database where records match conditions defined in the criteria range.

Creating Dynamic Dashboards

Dashboards are a visual representation of data, providing actionable insights at a glance. Excel's capacity for creating dynamic dashboards involves:

- **Data Validation**: Ensuring that your data inputs are correct and up to date.
- **PivotTables**: Using PivotTables to summarize data effectively.
- **Slicers and Timelines**: Implementing slicers and timelines for interactive data exploration.
- **Charts and Graphs**: Customizing charts and graphs that update dynamically with the underlying data.

Implementing Form Controls

Form controls in Excel, such as drop-down lists, option buttons, and sliders, enhance data interaction, making dashboards more interactive and user-friendly.

- **Integration**: Link form controls to cell values which act as inputs for database queries within your Excel models.

Best Practices for Utilizing Advanced Database Techniques

To effectively implement and use advanced database techniques in Excel 2024, consider the following strategies:

- **Normalize Your Data**: Before you start working with complex data, ensure that it is normalized. This means structuring your database to reduce redundancy and dependency, which optimizes the integrity of your data queries.
- **Use Tables for Data Management**: Convert ranges into tables (using the **Create Table** feature). Tables in Excel are powerful as they allow for easier data manipulation, formula application, and referencing.
- **Leverage SQL Queries with Power Query**: For users needing to execute more complex queries, Power Query offers integration with SQL, providing a familiar and robust query language capable of handling sophisticated data operations.
- **Maintain Data Integrity**: Validate data inputs through data validation rules, ensuring that the data used in your calculations and reports remains accurate and consistent.

Mastering advanced database techniques in Excel 2024 transforms the platform from a mere spreadsheet tool into a powerful database management system. These advanced capabilities enable users to handle large datasets with agility and precision, perform complex calculations, and present data in insightful and interactive ways.

Whether you're a financial analyst needing to perform yearly revenue forecasts, a marketing professional analyzing consumer data, or a human resources manager overseeing employee information, Excel's advanced database functions are indispensable tools in your data management arsenal. By understanding and applying these techniques, you can turn vast data into valuable insights, driving better decision-making and business strategies.

10. MACROS AND AUTOMATION

RECORDING MACROS

In the dynamic realm of Excel 2024, the ability to record macros serves as a powerful bridge between routine tasks and automation, transforming repetitive actions into simple, single-click solutions. Macros are not merely shortcuts; they are custom scripts that perform functions across your data, driving efficiency and consistency in your workflows.

The Power of Recording Macros

Macros in Excel are based on Visual Basic for Applications (VBA), a programming language that allows you to automate almost any aspect of Excel. By recording a macro, you're instructing Excel to capture a series of commands and operations so that they can be replayed or executed at a later time with the same exactitude.

Getting Started with Macro Recording

Recording a macro is akin to teaching Excel exactly what you want it to do. Here is how you can start automating your tasks:

Step 1: Prepare Your Data

Before you record a macro, ensure your dataset is well-organized. Macros will perform actions exactly as recorded, so any disorganization or errors in your initial setup could be replicated.

Step 2: Access the Developer Tab

The Developer tab is not visible by default in Excel. To add it to the ribbon:

- Go to **File > Options > Customize Ribbon**.
- Check the box labeled **Developer** and click **OK**.

Step 3: Record the Macro

1. **Initiate Recording**: On the Developer tab, click **Record Macro**.
2. **Set Macro Details**:
   - **Name your macro**: Use a short, descriptive name without spaces.
   - **Assign a shortcut key**: This can be any letter/combination that, when pressed with Ctrl, will start your macro.
   - **Store macro in**: Decide whether the macro should be available only in the current workbook (**This Workbook**) or all workbooks (**Personal Macro Workbook**).
   - **Description**: Add a brief description of what the macro does.

3. **Perform the tasks**: Carry out the steps you want to automate, such as formatting cells, entering formulas, or setting up data filters.
4. **Stop Recording**: Go back to the Developer tab and click **Stop Recording**.

Tips for Effective Macro Recording

- **Plan Your Steps**: Before recording, plan out the sequence of actions to ensure smooth and efficient execution.
- **Keep It Simple**: Avoid overly complex sequences in a single macro. Break down tasks into manageable actions to avoid errors.
- **Test Your Macro**: After recording, test the macro on a sample dataset to ensure it performs as expected.

Practical Applications of Macros

Macros can significantly enhance productivity in various scenarios:

- **Data Entry and Formatting**: Automate repetitive tasks like entering date stamps, formatting reports, or applying consistent cell styles across multiple sheets.
- **Data Analysis**: Automate complex calculations and data transformations that need to be performed routinely, ensuring accuracy and saving time.
- **Reporting**: Generate standardized reports, including formatting, headings, and calculations, ready for presentation or further analysis.

Advanced Macro Techniques

As you become more comfortable with recording basic macros, you may start exploring more advanced techniques:

- **Editing Macros**: Recorded macros can be edited in the VBA editor to refine their functionality or extend their capabilities.

- **Combining Macros with Formulas**: Integrate Excel functions into your macros to enhance their utility, making them not only automate tasks but also perform conditional operations based on the data they process.

Recording macros in Excel 2024 offers a pathway to elevating your efficiency, allowing you to focus more on strategic tasks while leaving the repetitive, time-consuming processes to be handled automatically. As you explore the depths of macro functionality, you transform your use of Excel from a manual data manipulation tool into an automated data handling powerhouse.

By mastering macros, you not only save time but also bolster the reliability and consistency of your data operations, paving the way for more advanced uses of Excel in your professional environment.

BASIC VBA CODING

Venturing into the realm of VBA (Visual Basic for Applications) in Excel 2024 is akin to discovering a hidden layer beneath the surface of Excel's robust functionality—a layer where the potential to automate, customize, and optimize your data interactions becomes boundless. VBA coding is the backbone of automation in Excel, enabling users to transcend the limitations of standard formulas and functions by crafting tailored macro scripts that can manipulate data in sophisticated ways.

Introduction to Basic VBA Coding

VBA in Excel is a powerful scripting language that allows you to automate repetitive tasks and create complex workflows. Whether you're generating customized reports, managing user interactions, or automating data entry and analysis, VBA provides the tools to create solutions that are both efficient and scalable.

Setting Up Your VBA Environment

Before you dive into writing VBA code, you need to familiarize yourself with the VBA Editor:

1. **Access the VBA Editor**: Press **ALT + F11** to open the VBA Editor.
2. **Explore the Interface**: The VBA Editor window consists of a menu bar, toolbar, Project Explorer, Properties window, and a central area to write and view code.

Writing Your First Macro in VBA

Creating your first VBA macro involves several key steps, designed to introduce you to the basics of VBA coding:

1. Create a New Module

- In the VBA Editor, right-click on **VBAProject (YourWorkbookName.xlsm)** in the Project Explorer.
- Select **Insert > Module** to add a new module where you will write your code.

2. Define a Subroutine

- Start by typing **Sub** followed by the name of your macro, for example, **Sub MyFirstMacro()**.
- Press **Enter**, and the VBA editor will automatically add **End Sub** to denote the end of your macro.

3. Write Simple VBA Code

- Inside the subroutine, write a simple VBA statement, like:

```
MsgBox "Hello, Excel World!"
```

This line of code creates a message box that will display when the macro is run.

4. Run Your Macro

- Place the cursor anywhere within your subroutine code.
- Press **F5** to run the macro, or go to **Run > Run Sub/UserForm** from the menu.

Basic VBA Concepts

Understanding a few fundamental concepts can help you navigate the basics of VBA coding more effectively:

Variables and Data Types

- Declare variables to store data temporarily. For example:

```
Dim myNumber As Integer
myNumber = 10
```

Use different data types (Integer, String, Boolean, etc.) based on the nature of data you are dealing with.

Control Structures

- Incorporate decision-making into your macros with **If...Else** statements:

```
If myNumber > 5 Then
    MsgBox "Large Number"
Else
    MsgBox "Small Number"
End If
```

Use loops to repeat actions. For example, a **For** loop:

```
For i = 1 To 5
    MsgBox "Iteration " & i
Next i
```

Debugging VBA Code

- **Immediate Window**: Use the Immediate Window (View > Immediate Window) to test lines of code on the fly.
- **Breakpoints**: Set breakpoints by clicking in the margin next to a line of code to pause execution at that point.
- **Step Through**: Use the **F8** key to step through your code line by line to observe behavior and track variable values.

Best Practices for Learning VBA

- **Start Small**: Begin with small, simple scripts to build your understanding and confidence.
- **Comment Your Code**: Always comment your code to explain what each section does, making it easier for you or others to understand later.
- **Practice Regularly**: Like any language, proficiency in VBA comes from practice. Try automating small, routine tasks you encounter to improve your skills.

Delving into VBA coding opens up a new dimension of possibilities within Excel 2024. As you learn to write basic VBA code, you gradually begin to unlock the full potential of Excel, transforming it from a mere spreadsheet tool into a powerful engine for data management and analysis. This journey not only enhances your productivity but also expands your analytical capabilities, allowing you to automate complex tasks and solve challenging problems efficiently.

AUTOMATING TASKS

In the advanced corridors of Excel 2024, automating tasks is akin to setting the gears of a well-oiled machine into motion, where each task, no matter how monotonous or complex, is executed with precision and efficiency. Automation not only expedites workflows but also minimizes the risk of human errors, thereby enhancing productivity and allowing users to focus on more strategic activities. This transformation from manual to automated processes is pivotal in today's data-driven environments, where time is often as valuable as the information being processed.

The Art of Automation in Excel

Automation in Excel involves the use of macros, VBA (Visual Basic for Applications) scripts, and built-in features that together form a powerful arsenal capable of handling a wide array of tasks ranging from simple data entries to complex analytical reports.

Leveraging Macros for Task Automation

Macros are one of the simplest forms of automation in Excel. They record a sequence of actions to perform tasks such as formatting data, creating charts, or setting up complex calculations which can then be executed with a single command.

- **Macro Recorder**: Start with the macro recorder for basic tasks. It captures your actions as you perform them in Excel and converts these actions into a VBA script.
- **Triggering Macros**: Assign macros to buttons, images, or even a shortcut key, making the execution as easy as a click or a keystroke.

Introducing VBA for Advanced Automation

While the macro recorder is useful for straightforward tasks, learning VBA opens up a broader range of automation possibilities. VBA allows for conditional logic, looping, and interaction with Excel's object model, which means you can automate virtually any aspect of Excel's functionality.

- **Automating Reports**: Use VBA to pull data from external sources, apply calculations, and format the results in a report layout automatically.
- **Data Management**: Write VBA scripts to sort data, merge data from multiple sheets, clean up data, or automate the creation of pivot tables.

Practical Applications of Excel Automation

Automating tasks in Excel can significantly enhance efficiency in various operational aspects:

- **Financial Modeling**: Automate the retrieval and consolidation of financial data from different sources and run complex financial models automatically.

- **Inventory Tracking**: Set up an automated system to track inventory levels, reorder statuses, and generate restocking alerts.

- **Performance Dashboards**: Develop dynamic dashboards that update automatically with real-time data, providing continuous insights into business or project performance.

Steps to Automate an Excel Task

To effectively automate a task in Excel, follow these structured steps:

1. **Define the Task**: Clearly define what needs to be automated. Understand every step of the process to ensure that nothing is overlooked during automation.

2. **Record or Write the Script**: Use the macro recorder for basic tasks or write a custom VBA script for more complex processes.

3. **Test the Automation**: Run your macro or script in a test environment first. Check for any errors or unintended outcomes and refine the script as necessary.

4. **Implement Triggers**: Decide how the automated tasks will be triggered. This could be through a button on the sheet, a specific event in Excel, or scheduled timing.

5. **Document the Process**: Provide documentation for the automated process, detailing how it works and any manual steps that might still be necessary.

Best Practices for Automating Tasks in Excel

- **Keep Automation Simple**: Start with simple tasks to build confidence and understanding. Complex automations can be broken down into smaller, manageable tasks.

- **Maintain Clarity in Code**: Use comments in your VBA scripts to explain what each section of the code does. This is crucial for maintaining or modifying the code later.

- **Stay Informed on Excel Updates**: New versions of Excel may offer additional automation features or changes to existing ones. Keeping updated can help you make the most of Excel's capabilities.

Automation in Excel is not just about saving time; it's about enhancing accuracy, reliability, and the capability to handle data at scale. As you delve deeper into Excel's automation tools, you unlock new levels of productivity and analytical power, allowing you to focus on insights and decision-making rather than mundane processes. In the landscape of modern data management, proficiency in automating Excel tasks is an invaluable skill, propelling your capabilities from basic data handling to strategic data orchestration.

11. POWER PIVOT AND ADVANCED DATA MODELING

POWER PIVOT INTRODUCTION

In the contemporary tableau of Excel 2024, Power Pivot stands as a formidable extension, transforming Excel from a traditional spreadsheet tool into a powerful data modeling and analytical engine. This profound transformation enables users to manage large datasets with the efficiency and sophistication of a relational database right within Excel, combining the user-friendly interface of Excel with the robust power of advanced data manipulation and analysis.

The Genesis of Power Pivot

Introduced as an add-in for earlier versions of Excel, Power Pivot has evolved into a core feature, integral for users who need to perform complex data analysis and create extensive data models. Power Pivot provides advanced data modeling features, such as creating relationships between heterogeneous data, building complex calculations, and designing intricate Key Performance Indicators (KPIs) directly within Excel.

Enabling Power Pivot in Excel 2024

To dive into the capabilities of Power Pivot, you first need to ensure it is enabled in your version of Excel:

1. **Access Excel Options**: Click on **File**, then **Options**, and go to the **Add-Ins** category.
2. **Manage Add-Ins**: At the bottom of the window, in the **Manage** box, select **COM Add-ins** and click **Go**.
3. **Enable Power Pivot**: In the list of available COM Add-Ins, check the box next to **Microsoft Power Pivot for Excel** and then click **OK**.

Once enabled, Power Pivot adds a new tab in the Excel ribbon, opening up a suite of powerful data analysis tools.

Core Features of Power Pivot

Data Model Creation

Power Pivot allows you to import and integrate data from various sources, including databases, data feeds, Excel files, and even cloud-based data. Once imported, you can manage this data in the Power Pivot window, where you can:

- **Create Relationships**: Like a relational database, Power Pivot lets you define relationships between different tables of data without needing to use complex VLOOKUPs or INDEX/MATCH formulas.
- **Add Calculated Columns**: Use DAX (Data Analysis Expressions) to create new data columns calculated from other columns in your data model.

DAX: The Formula Language

DAX is a formula language specifically designed for data modeling. It extends the capabilities of Excel formulas in the context of data manipulation and querying:

- **Basic DAX Syntax**: Similar to Excel formulas but designed to work with tables and columns.
- **Measures**: DAX allows you to create measures (dynamic calculations) that are used in PivotTables and PivotCharts. These are powerful for creating dynamic aggregations.

Implementing a Simple Power Pivot Model

To understand the power of Power Pivot, consider a scenario where you need to analyze sales data from multiple regions, each stored in different tables:

1. **Import Data**: Use the Power Pivot window to import all relevant tables.
2. **Create Relationships**: Define relationships between your sales data and other dimension tables like dates, products, and regions using the drag-and-drop interface in the diagram view.
3. **Develop Measures**: Create measures to calculate total sales, average sales, and other metrics using DAX formulas.

Visualizing Data with Power Pivot

Once your data model is set up, you can use it to power PivotTables and PivotCharts within Excel. These visualizations can be refreshingly dynamic and responsive, updating instantly as your data model changes.

- **Slicers and Timelines**: Enhance your PivotTables and PivotCharts by adding slicers and timelines for easy filtering and time-based analysis.

Best Practices When Using Power Pivot

- **Plan Your Data Model**: Before building your model, plan out the tables, relationships, and calculations you will need.
- **Keep Data Clean**: Ensure your data is clean and well-prepared before importing it into Power Pivot to avoid complications in relationships and calculations.
- **Learn DAX**: Invest time in learning DAX to fully utilize the capabilities of Power Pivot. DAX can be complex, but it is incredibly powerful once mastered.

Power Pivot is not merely an add-in; it is a gateway to advanced data analysis within Excel, combining the simplicity of Excel with the power of a data processing engine. By harnessing the capabilities of Power Pivot, you elevate your analytical prowess to new heights, enabling you to handle and analyze data in ways that were previously possible only with specialized software. Whether you're a financial analyst, a marketing researcher, or a data scientist, Power Pivot equips you with the tools to turn data into insights and insights into action.

BUILDING DATA MODELS

In the advanced landscape of Excel 2024, the ability to build robust data models using Power Pivot is a game-changer for users who need to manage, analyze, and visualize large datasets effectively. A data model in Power Pivot isn't just a collection of tables and relationships; it is a sophisticated framework designed to turn extensive raw data into meaningful information, providing a foundation for in-depth analysis and decision-making.

Understanding Data Models

A data model in Power Pivot enables you to integrate data from various sources, ranging from different Excel sheets to external databases, and to organize this data into a structured form. It includes tables, relationships, and metadata that can be used in your analyses. By effectively building a data model, you can analyze large amounts of data efficiently without impacting Excel's performance.

Steps to Build a Data Model in Power Pivot

Building a data model in Excel 2024 involves several critical steps, each designed to ensure your model is both scalable and powerful.

1. Importing Data

Power Pivot allows you to import data from a variety of sources. This can include SQL databases, Excel files, text files, and more. The first step in building your model is to bring all the necessary data into Power Pivot.

- **Data Import Wizard**: Use the Power Pivot window to access the Home tab, and then click on 'Manage Data Model'. Here, you can import data through the Table Import Wizard.
- **Consider Data Types and Volume**: Ensure you understand the types and volumes of data you are importing, as this will influence the design of your model.

2. Defining Relationships

Once your data is imported, the next step is to define relationships between your tables. Power Pivot does not require all data to be contained in a single table; instead, it can create relationships between multiple tables.

- **Creating Relationships**: In the Power Pivot window, use the Diagram View to drag and drop fields between tables to create relationships. This could be linking a Sales table's Product ID to a Product table's Product ID.
- **Understanding Relationship Types**: Ensure you understand one-to-many or many-to-one relationships, as these will impact how data is aggregated and analyzed in your model.

3. Adding Calculations

You can enhance your data model with calculations that can be reused in multiple reports and analyses across your workbook.

- **Calculated Columns**: Use DAX to create new columns in your tables, which calculate values based on existing data in your model.
- **Measures**: These are calculations used in reporting and analysis, such as sums, averages, minimums, and maximums, which you define using DAX.

4. Optimizing and Managing the Data Model

A well-optimized data model provides quicker access to data and more efficient analyses.

- **Manage and Optimize Data**: Regularly review your data model for any unnecessary columns or data that may slow down processing. Use the Advanced tab in Power Pivot to manage data refreshes and optimize how data is loaded.

- **Use Hierarchies**: Build hierarchies in your data model to enable users to drill down into data during analysis, which is particularly useful in pivot tables and reports.

Best Practices for Data Modeling

- **Keep Your Model Relevant**: Only include data in your model that is necessary for analysis to maintain performance and relevance.
- **Document Your Model**: Maintain documentation that describes the sources, relationships, and key calculations within your model. This is crucial for maintenance and future modifications.
- **Regularly Update and Refine**: As business needs change, regularly update and refine your data model to reflect new requirements or data sources.

Building data models in Power Pivot within Excel 2024 empowers users to handle complex data scenarios more effectively, turning vast amounts of data into actionable insights. These models serve as the backbone for advanced analysis, enabling businesses to perform high-level analytics that are integral to strategic decision-making. By mastering the art of data modeling in Power Pivot, you elevate your analytical capabilities, enhancing your proficiency in navigating the data-driven challenges of the modern world.

DAX FUNDAMENTALS

In the sophisticated realm of Excel 2024's Power Pivot, mastering Data Analysis Expressions (DAX) is akin to learning the language that bridges the gap between raw data and actionable insights. DAX is a formula language specifically designed for enhanced data manipulation and analysis in Excel's Power Pivot and Power BI tools. Understanding DAX is crucial for anyone looking to delve deeper into the functionalities that Excel offers beyond conventional formulas, enabling the creation of advanced business intelligence solutions directly within Excel.

Introduction to DAX Fundamentals

DAX includes functions, operators, and constants that can be used in a formula, or expression, to calculate and return one or more values. Stepping into DAX can seem daunting due to its complexity and its powerful capabilities in handling data. However, by breaking down its fundamentals, you can begin to harness its potential effectively.

Core Concepts of DAX

DAX formulas are designed to work with data that is stored in tables. Unlike standard Excel formulas, which focus on operating on individual cell values, DAX allows you to perform data manipulation at a higher level—focusing on columns and rows within entire tables.

1. Understanding Context in DAX

One of the most critical concepts in DAX is context. Context in DAX dictates how data values are evaluated and displayed in different scenarios:

- **Row Context**: This is where calculations are performed row by row, across a table. It's common within calculated columns.
- **Filter Context**: This affects calculations that aggregate data, like sums or averages. It can be influenced by filters applied to reports, like slicers or PivotTable filters.

2. Basic Syntax and Functions

DAX functions often resemble Excel functions but are designed to work within the aforementioned contexts. Here's a brief overview of some basic yet powerful DAX functions:

- **CALCULATE**: Adjusts the context in which a data expression is evaluated. It is one of the most powerful functions in DAX and pivotal in many advanced data scenarios.

```
CALCULATE(SUM(Orders[Amount]), Orders[Year] = "2024")
```

SUM, AVERAGE, MIN, MAX: These aggregate functions work similar to their Excel counterparts but are used over columns from a related table or filter.

- **RELATED**: Retrieves a value from another table that is related to the current table.

```
RELATED(Product[ProductName])
```

Building Formulas in DAX

Creating formulas in DAX involves understanding the data model—its tables, relationships, and the specific business logic relevant to your analysis. Here are steps to construct effective DAX formulas:

1. **Define Your Goal**: Clearly understand what you are trying to calculate or analyze.
2. **Identify Tables and Relationships**: Ensure you know how your tables are related and how data flows between them.
3. **Write the Formula**: Start with simple formulas to get a feel for syntax and function, then move to more complex calculations as needed.
4. **Test and Refine**: Always test your formulas to make sure they behave as expected in different scenarios.

Practical Applications of DAX

- **Time Intelligence**: DAX provides powerful time intelligence functions, like **DATEADD** and **SAMEPERIODLASTYEAR**, to make calculations over time easy.
- **Dynamic Reporting**: Use DAX to create dynamic reports that adjust and recalibrate as your data changes or as filters are applied.
- **Complex Business Rules**: Implement complex business logic into your data model for in-depth analyses, such as conditional calculations and multi-table aggregations.

Best Practices for Learning DAX

- **Start Small**: Begin with basic functions and gradually incorporate more complex formulas as you grow comfortable.
- **Use Resources**: Utilize books, online tutorials, and community forums dedicated to DAX and Power Pivot.
- **Practice Regularly**: Like any language, DAX requires practice. Try to apply what you learn in real-world scenarios.

DAX is not just a tool; it's a critical skill set for any data professional using Excel 2024 who needs to perform advanced data manipulation and analysis efficiently. Understanding DAX means you can transform extensive and complex data into insightful, actionable information. With DAX, Excel is no longer just a spreadsheet application; it's a powerful engine for data analysis, capable of supporting complex business intelligence tasks directly on your desktop.

12. Creating Interactive Dashboards

Dashboard Planning

In the world of data analytics within Excel 2024, crafting an interactive dashboard is much like constructing a vital bridge between vast data reserves and the actionable insights they hold. This bridge, when carefully planned and constructed, enables stakeholders to view, understand, and interact with complex data sets effortlessly. A well-designed dashboard not only displays data but also tells a story, guiding the user through data-driven narratives that drive strategic decisions.

The Essence of Dashboard Planning

Dashboard planning is a critical phase where the groundwork for effective data visualization and interaction is laid. This stage determines not only how the data will be presented but also how it will be perceived and utilized by its audience.

1. Define the Purpose and Audience

The first step in dashboard planning involves defining the dashboard's purpose and identifying its primary audience. Understanding who will use the dashboard and what they need to achieve with it guides the design and functionality:

- **Operational Dashboards**: Focus on real-time data to monitor daily operations.
- **Analytical Dashboards**: Provide deeper insights into data for strategic decision-making.

2. Determine Key Performance Indicators (KPIs)

Identifying the right KPIs is crucial as they will drive the focus of the dashboard. KPIs should align with the strategic goals of the organization and the specific objectives of the dashboard's users. They should be actionable, regularly measurable, and provide clear indications of performance.

3. Data Sources and Quality

Evaluate and identify the data sources that will feed into the dashboard. Data quality must be assessed to ensure reliability:

- **Accuracy and Relevance**: Data should be error-free and relevant to the KPIs.
- **Timeliness**: Ensure the data is up-to-date and can be refreshed at appropriate intervals.
- **Integration**: Data may need to be pulled from various sources; ensure it can be seamlessly integrated and standardized.

Planning the Dashboard Layout

The layout of the dashboard is where form meets function. It determines how effectively the information is communicated to the user.

4. Sketch the Layout

Start with a basic sketch or wireframe of the dashboard layout:

- **Grid Layout**: Plan your dashboard on a grid to balance the visual elements evenly.
- **Visual Hierarchy**: Place the most important information or KPIs centrally or at the top where viewers will naturally look first.
- **Navigation**: If the dashboard spans multiple pages or sections, plan for intuitive navigation.

5. Choose the Right Visualization Tools

Selecting the appropriate charts and graphs is key to effective data presentation:

- **Bar Charts**: Good for comparisons.
- **Line Graphs**: Effective for showing trends over time.
- **Heat Maps**: Useful for highlighting variations across categories or time.
- **PivotTables**: Allow dynamic interaction with the data for detailed analysis.

Interactive Elements and Functionality

Interactivity enhances the user experience by allowing users to engage with the data actively:

6. Implement Controls

Incorporate interactive controls like slicers, dropdown menus, or checkboxes that enable users to customize the data display according to their needs.

7. Tooltips and Drill-Downs

- **Tooltips**: Offer more detailed data and insights when hovering over parts of the dashboard.
- **Drill-Down Capability**: Allows users to click on elements of the dashboard to view more granular data.

Testing and Feedback

Before full deployment, the dashboard should undergo rigorous testing:

8. User Testing

Conduct testing with a small group of end users to gather feedback on the dashboard's usability and functionality. This feedback is invaluable in refining the dashboard.

9. Iteration and Improvement

Based on feedback, make necessary adjustments to improve both performance and user satisfaction.

Planning an interactive dashboard in Excel 2024 is a meticulous process that combines art with analytics. It requires a deep understanding of the audience's needs, a strategic approach to data presentation, and a thoughtful integration of interactive elements. By following a structured planning process, you ensure that your dashboard not only meets but exceeds the expectations of its users, providing them with a powerful tool to visualize, understand, and make informed decisions based on their data.

VISUALIZING DATA WITH PIVOTCHARTS

In the digital age, where data is as rich and complex as ever, PivotCharts in Excel 2024 serve as essential tools for translating this vast information into clear, actionable visual insights. PivotCharts extend the functionality of PivotTables by adding the visual dimension necessary for intuitive and immediate comprehension of trends, patterns, and outliers within large datasets. This ability to visualize data effectively not only enhances understanding but also aids in communicating complex information succinctly and persuasively to diverse audiences.

The Strategic Role of PivotCharts in Data Visualization

PivotCharts are more than just a means of creating appealing graphics. They are strategic tools that allow users to dynamically interact with their data through drilling down, slicing, dicing, and even exploring what-if scenarios in real-time. This level of interactivity is indispensable for users who need to explore nuances and derive specific insights from aggregated data.

Creating Your First PivotChart

The process of creating a PivotChart in Excel 2024 mirrors the ease and flexibility of building PivotTables, but with an added layer of visual output:

Step 1: Select Your Data

Like any data visualization tool, the first step is to ensure your data is well-organized and formatted. Ideally, your data should be in a tabular format, with clear headings for each column.

Step 2: Insert a PivotChart

Navigate to the "Insert" tab on the Excel ribbon and select "PivotChart." Excel will prompt you to select your data range and choose whether you want the PivotChart placed in a new worksheet or an existing one.

Step 3: Define the PivotChart Fields

- **Choose Fields**: Drag and drop fields into the PivotChart field areas—Axis (Categories), Legend (Series), and Values. Your selections will determine how data is grouped and summarized visually.
- **Configure Fields**: Depending on the field's role in your PivotChart, you might configure additional options like summing values, counting items, or calculating averages.

Best Practices for Designing PivotCharts

Creating effective PivotCharts involves more than just understanding the technical steps. It requires an eye for design and a strategic understanding of data presentation:

Choose chart types that clearly represent your data. While Excel offers a variety of chart styles—bar, line, area, pie, scatter, and more—selecting the right type depends on what best communicates your data's story.

Avoid clutter. Simplify your charts by removing unnecessary labels, legends, or gridlines that do not provide additional insight. This focus on simplicity helps in maintaining the audience's attention on the most critical data points.

Color is a powerful tool in visualization but should be used judiciously. Use color to highlight significant data points or trends and maintain a consistent color scheme that aligns with your organization's or your presentation's theme.

Interactive Features of PivotCharts

One of the key strengths of PivotCharts is their ability to become highly interactive and dynamic:

Slicers

Add slicers to your PivotCharts to make them more interactive. Slicers act as filters that viewers can use to segment the data dynamically within the chart. This feature is particularly useful during presentations or when sharing reports with stakeholders who might want to explore different facets of the data.

Timelines

For datasets that include dates, adding a timeline can enhance user interaction, allowing for easy filtering of data across different time periods directly from the chart interface.

Drill-down Capabilities

Excel 2024 allows users to drill down into their PivotChart elements. This means viewers can click on a chart element to see more granular data related to that element—a powerful feature for deep dives into data.

PivotCharts in Excel 2024 are not just about visualizing data—they are about bringing data to life, making it speak in the most compelling and understandable way possible. They empower users to see beyond the numbers, to uncover patterns and insights that might otherwise remain hidden in raw datasets. By mastering PivotCharts, you equip yourself with the ability to not only analyze data comprehensively but also to share and communicate these insights effectively, ensuring that your data-driven stories make an impact.

ADDING INTERACTIVITY WITH SLICERS AND TIMELINES

In the realm of data analysis and visualization, the dynamic interactivity offered by Excel 2024 elevates user engagement and data exploration to new heights. Slicers and Timelines, two pivotal features of Excel, are not merely aesthetic enhancements; they are powerful tools that allow users to interact with data directly, filtering and viewing specific segments without altering underlying datasets. This sub-chapter delves into how incorporating these tools can transform static data into interactive, dynamic dashboards that enhance decision-making processes.

Introduction to Slicers and Timelines

Slicers and Timelines enhance the interactive capabilities of Excel dashboards by providing an intuitive and visual way of filtering data that is both accessible to beginners and powerful enough for advanced users. They make it possible for any user to drill down into specifics with just a few clicks, turning complex data sets into understandable and actionable insights.

Understanding Slicers

Slicers are graphical filtering controls that allow users to quickly and easily filter the data displayed in PivotTables and PivotCharts. Unlike traditional filters that are hidden away in drop-down menus, slicers are laid out prominently on the spreadsheet, inviting interaction.

- **Setup**: To add a slicer, simply click on your PivotTable or PivotChart, navigate to the "Analyze" or "PivotTable Analyze" tab on the Ribbon, and select "Insert Slicer." Choose the data categories you want to include as slicers, and they will appear as buttons on your worksheet.
- **Customization**: Slicers can be customized for color, size, and number of columns to fit the layout of your dashboard, making them not only functional but also visually appealing.

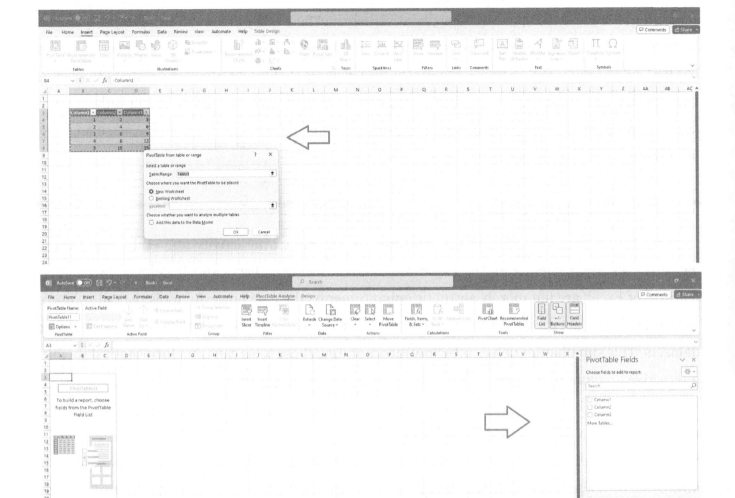

Exploring Timelines

Timelines are a specialized type of slicer exclusively designed for filtering dates. They provide a simple, graphical way to add date filters linked to your data model and are especially useful when dealing with trends over time.

- **Implementation**: Like slicers, Timelines are added via the "Insert Timeline" button found under the "PivotTable Analyze" tab when a PivotTable or PivotChart is selected. You must have date fields in your data model to use Timelines.

- **Functionality**: Timelines allow for easy selection of time periods through a slider bar, enabling quick views of data across different time segments—year, quarter, month, or day.

Practical Applications of Slicers and Timelines

Integrating slicers and timelines into your Excel dashboards enables a more interactive data exploration experience. Here's how they can be used effectively:

Data Comparison

By selecting different filters on slicers or adjusting the range in timelines, users can compare how different segments of data change over time or under different conditions. This is invaluable for identifying trends, anomalies, or patterns.

Slicers and timelines improve user engagement by allowing users to interact with the data themselves. This hands-on interaction is not only more engaging but also allows users to explore the data in a way that suits their specific needs or questions.

For dashboards that are linked to dynamically updating data sources, slicers and timelines allow for real-time data analysis. Users can adjust their views and analyses based on the most current data available.

Best Practices for Using Slicers and Timelines

To maximize the effectiveness of slicers and timelines in your Excel dashboards, consider the following best practices:

- **Consistent Formatting**: Ensure that the style and format of your slicers and timelines are consistent with the overall design of your dashboard. Consistency helps in maintaining an intuitive and professional appearance.
- **Clear Labeling**: Label your slicers and timelines clearly so users understand what data they are interacting with. This is crucial for dashboards that will be used by people who may not be familiar with the dataset.
- **Strategic Placement**: Place slicers and timelines near the data they influence. This spatial correlation helps users intuitively understand what parts of the dashboard are being controlled by their interactions.

Slicers and timelines are more than just tools for filtering data—they are gateways to a deeper understanding and a more profound engagement with the information your dashboard presents. By incorporating these interactive elements into your Excel dashboards, you empower users to explore and interact with data on their terms, leading to more insightful analyses and informed decisions. Whether for business intelligence, financial analysis, or academic research, slicers and timelines transform the way we interact with and perceive data in Excel 2024.

PART IV: EXCEL FOR PROFESSIONALS

13. COLLABORATION AND SECURITY

SHARING WORKBOOKS AND REAL-TIME COLLABORATION

In today's interconnected world, the ability to share workbooks and collaborate in real-time within Excel 2024 has become more than just a feature—it's a necessity. This capability transforms Excel from a personal analysis tool into a dynamic platform where teams can work together across different geographies in real time, ensuring that all stakeholders are on the same page, literally and figuratively. This collaborative power of Excel ensures that it remains an indispensable tool in the modern professional landscape, enhancing productivity, improving accuracy, and accelerating decision-making processes.

The Importance of Workbook Sharing and Collaboration

Sharing and collaboration in Excel allow multiple users to view, edit, and update workbooks simultaneously. This functionality is crucial for projects where team members must work together to compile data, analyze trends, and generate reports. It ensures that everyone has access to the latest data, helping to avoid the confusion and errors that can arise from multiple versions of a document.

Setting Up Excel for Real-Time Collaboration
Enabling Sharing in Excel

To begin sharing a workbook in Excel 2024, you need to save it to a location accessible to all collaborators, such as OneDrive, SharePoint, or a similar cloud service. This setup allows multiple users to access the workbook simultaneously:

1. **Save Your Workbook Online**: Save your document to a cloud service. This is a prerequisite for enabling real-time collaboration.
2. **Invite Collaborators**: Once your workbook is online, you can share it by inviting others via email or a sharing link. Excel allows you to control whether recipients can edit or only view the workbook.

Collaborating in Real-Time

Once shared, collaborators can open the workbook simultaneously. Changes made by any user are instantly visible to all others, with each collaborator's cursor and selections highlighted in a unique color:

- **Seeing Changes**: Excel displays a flag in cells that are being edited by another user, showing who is making the change.
- **Communication Tools**: Utilize integrated chat functions (if using Office 365) or comments and notes within the workbook to communicate changes, queries, or updates.

Best Practices for Sharing Workbooks and Collaborating

Effective collaboration in Excel requires more than just the technical setup. Following these best practices can help ensure that collaboration is smooth and productive:

- **Establish Guidelines**: Define clear guidelines for how the workbook should be used and edited. Decide who is responsible for inputting data, who can approve changes, and how conflicts will be resolved.
- **Track Changes**: Use Excel's built-in "Track Changes" feature to monitor who made what changes and when. This can be crucial for maintaining data integrity and understanding the evolution of the workbook.
- **Regular Updates and Syncs**: Ensure that all collaborators keep their software up to date and regularly sync their changes to avoid conflicts or data loss.
- **Use Data Validation**: Implement data validation rules to maintain data integrity across multiple users. This helps prevent entry errors and ensures that the data remains reliable and accurate.

Leveraging Advanced Collaboration Features

Excel 2024 offers advanced features that can enhance collaborative efforts:

- **Co-Authoring**: This feature allows multiple users to work on a document simultaneously. It's especially useful for teams spread across different locations.
- **Version History**: Access to version history allows users to view previous versions of the workbook, which is invaluable for understanding changes over time and restoring previous states if needed.

Sharing workbooks and collaborating in real-time are pivotal in leveraging the full potential of Excel 2024 for professional use.

These capabilities transform how teams interact with data, making workflows more efficient and decision-making faster. By embracing these features, professionals can enhance their productivity and ensure that their teams are more aligned and informed, no matter where they are located. In essence, Excel's collaborative tools are not just about sharing data; they're about fostering teamwork and driving collective success.

DATA PROTECTION

In today's data-driven environment, the security and protection of data within Excel 2024 take precedence, especially for professionals who manage sensitive or confidential information. As the usage of Excel extends into the realms of finance, healthcare, and personal data, ensuring robust data protection is not just a recommended practice—it's an imperative. This sub-chapter explores the mechanisms Excel 2024 provides to safeguard data, ensuring that integrity and confidentiality are maintained, and regulatory requirements are met.

Understanding Data Protection in Excel

Data protection in Excel involves more than just safeguarding files against unauthorized access; it extends to preserving data integrity, preventing data loss, and managing user permissions effectively. Excel 2024 offers several features that support these aspects, tailored to meet the needs of professional environments where data breaches or leaks can have significant consequences.

Encrypting Workbooks

Encryption is the first line of defense in protecting sensitive data stored in Excel files. Encrypting a workbook ensures that its contents are secured with a password, making the data inaccessible to anyone who does not have the password.

- **Implementing Encryption**: Go to **File > Info > Protect Workbook > Encrypt with Password**. Upon selecting this option, you will be prompted to enter a password. Once set, the file is encrypted, and the password must be entered to open the workbook in the future.
- **Best Practices for Passwords**: Choose strong passwords that combine letters, numbers, and symbols. Keep passwords confidential and consider using a password manager to keep track of them.

Using Advanced Permissions

For workbooks stored on network drives or in the cloud, Excel 2024 integrates with Windows Information Protection (WIP) and other management tools that allow more granular control over who can access information and how they can interact with it.

- **Permissions Settings**: You can set permissions via the **File > Info > Protect Workbook** menu, selecting **Restrict Access**. Here, you can define who can view or edit the workbook. These settings are particularly useful in collaborative environments where different team members may need different levels of access to data.

- **Document Management Systems**: For enterprise users, integrating Excel with a document management system can provide advanced audit trails and version control, further enhancing data security.

Data Loss Prevention

To prevent accidental data exposure, Excel 2024 supports Data Loss Prevention (DLP) policies that can identify, monitor, and protect sensitive information within your documents.

- **Implementing DLP Policies**: These policies can be configured by IT administrators within your organization and might include rules to prevent the sharing of personally identifiable information (PII), financial data, or other sensitive information.

- **Alerts and Compliance**: When DLP policies are in place, Excel can provide real-time alerts if users attempt to save or share documents containing sensitive information in violation of established policies.

Sheet and Workbook Protection

Protecting specific components of an Excel file, such as sheets or the workbook structure, prevents unauthorized users from making changes to formulas, layouts, or key data.

- **Protecting Sheets**: Go to **Review > Protect Sheet** to lock certain actions in a worksheet. You can choose what users can and cannot do, such as inserting rows, deleting rows, or formatting cells.

- **Protecting Workbook Structure**: By choosing **Review > Protect Workbook**, you can prevent others from adding, moving, or deleting sheets within the workbook.

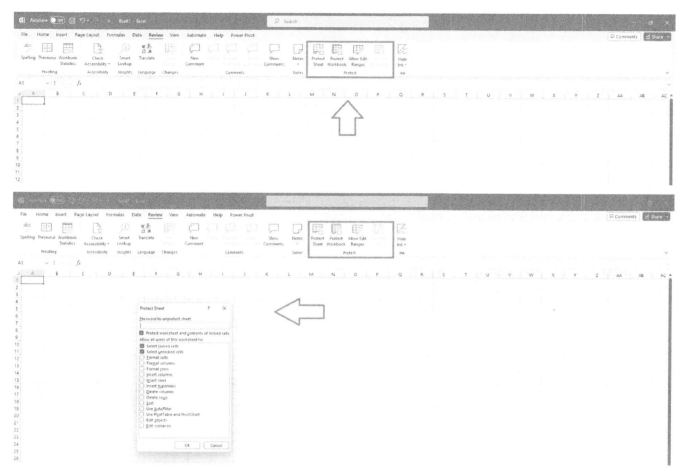

Audit Trails

Maintaining an audit trail is essential in environments where knowing who accessed a file and what changes were made is crucial for compliance and security.

- **Tracking Changes**: Excel's **Track Changes** feature can be turned on under the **Review** tab. This feature logs who made changes, what changes were made, and when they were made, providing a clear audit trail.

In Excel 2024, data protection extends beyond basic security measures, incorporating comprehensive tools that ensure data remains secure, private, and compliant with regulatory standards. By effectively utilizing encryption, permissions, DLP policies, and other protective features, professionals can safeguard their data against unauthorized access and potential breaches. This not only protects the organization's data assets but also reinforces its reputation as a trustworthy and secure handler of information.

CLOUD INTEGRATION

In the rapidly evolving landscape of modern business, the integration of cloud technology with Excel 2024 stands out as a transformative advancement. Cloud integration not only facilitates seamless collaboration and accessibility but also enhances security and scalability, enabling professionals to manage and analyze data more effectively than ever before. As businesses increasingly move towards digital and remote operations, the ability to integrate Excel with cloud services becomes a critical asset, empowering teams to work together from any location, on any device, with data synchronized in real time.

The Shift to Cloud-Enabled Excel

Cloud integration in Excel 2024 means more than just the ability to save files to a cloud service; it involves a comprehensive synchronization of data across platforms, real-time collaboration, and enhanced data security protocols that are managed through the cloud. This integration allows Excel to leverage the vast computational power and storage capabilities of cloud computing, making it immensely powerful for handling large datasets, complex analytics, and extensive reporting.

Benefits of Cloud Integration

Accessibility and Mobility

With Excel files hosted in the cloud, users can access their data anytime, anywhere, which is particularly beneficial for teams that are geographically dispersed. Whether it's updating a financial model from the office, analyzing sales data from home, or presenting quarterly reports on the go, cloud integration ensures that your important Excel workbooks are always accessible.

Enhanced Collaboration

Cloud integration transforms Excel into a dynamic workspace where multiple users can view and edit workbooks simultaneously. Changes made by one user are instantly visible to all others who have access, with changes tracked in real time. This capability not only speeds up the workflow but also ensures that everyone is always working with the most up-to-date information.

Data Security and Backup

Storing Excel workbooks in the cloud comes with enhanced security features provided by cloud service providers, including advanced encryption methods during transmission and at rest, regular security audits, and compliance with international data protection regulations. Additionally, cloud services often offer automated backup solutions, reducing the risk of data loss due to hardware failure, theft, or accidental deletion.

Implementing Cloud Integration in Excel

To fully integrate Excel 2024 with cloud computing, several steps and considerations must be addressed:

Choosing the Right Cloud Platform

Select a cloud platform that best fits your organizational needs. Options like Microsoft OneDrive, Google Drive, and Dropbox are popular for their robust features and seamless compatibility with Excel. Each platform offers different storage plans, security features, and collaboration tools, so choosing the right provider is crucial.

Setting Up Cloud Storage

1. **Create an Account**: Sign up for your chosen cloud service and set up an organizational account that can be accessed by all relevant team members.
2. **Install Necessary Apps**: Ensure that all team members have the required apps installed on their devices for accessing and syncing files.
3. **Upload Excel Files**: Move your Excel workbooks to the cloud. Most platforms offer a simple drag-and-drop interface for uploading files.

Integrating with Excel

1. **Link Excel with Your Cloud Account**: In Excel, go to **File > Account** and sign in with your cloud account. This will link Excel directly with your cloud storage.
2. **Save Workbooks to the Cloud**: When saving a new workbook, choose your cloud location as the destination. For existing workbooks, you can move them to the cloud by using the 'Save As' function and selecting your cloud drive.

Best Practices for Cloud Integration

- **Regularly Update Software**: Keep Excel and your cloud storage apps updated to the latest version to ensure you have the latest security patches and features.

- **Educate Your Team**: Conduct training sessions to educate your team on how to use cloud features effectively and securely.

- **Monitor Access and Activity**: Use the administrative tools provided by your cloud service to monitor who accesses your data and manage permissions appropriately.

Cloud integration with Excel 2024 marks a significant step forward in how professionals can manage and interact with data. By leveraging the power of the cloud, Excel becomes not just a tool for data analysis but a comprehensive platform for data management, collaboration, and security, capable of meeting the challenges of today's digital and globalized business environment. This integration enables businesses to harness the full potential of their data, driving insights and decisions that are informed, timely, and impactful.

14. EXCEL TIPS AND TRICKS

WORKFLOW OPTIMIZATION WITH SHORTCUTS

In the fast-paced world of modern business, efficiency is key. For professionals using Excel 2024, this means optimizing workflows not just through better data management and analysis techniques, but also by mastering the use of shortcuts. Shortcuts in Excel are not merely about saving time; they enhance productivity by reducing the repetitive strain of manual tasks and streamlining complex sequences of actions into simple keystrokes. This sub-chapter delves into how shortcuts can transform your interaction with Excel, making your workflow smoother and more efficient.

The Power of Keyboard Shortcuts in Excel

Keyboard shortcuts are critical for professionals who use Excel extensively. They allow you to perform actions quicker than using the mouse and can significantly speed up your data processing tasks. Understanding and utilizing these shortcuts can lead to a more streamlined, efficient use of Excel.

Fundamental Shortcuts for Everyday Tasks

Here are some essential shortcuts that every Excel user should know to enhance their daily productivity:

- **Ctrl + C, Ctrl + V, Ctrl + X**: These are the universal shortcuts for copy, paste, and cut, respectively, and they work seamlessly within Excel for moving data and formulas around your workbook.
- **Ctrl + Z, Ctrl + Y**: Undo and redo are invaluable for quickly correcting mistakes or redoing actions.
- **Ctrl + Arrow Keys**: Jump to the edge of data regions, which helps quickly navigate around large datasets without scrolling.
- **Alt + E, S, V**: This sequence opens the Paste Special dialog, which is a powerhouse for doing more complex paste operations like pasting values only or formatting.
- **Ctrl + Shift + L**: Toggle filters on and off for data ranges or tables, which is useful for quickly sorting through data points.

Advanced Shortcuts for Data Analysis

For those delving deeper into data analysis, these shortcuts can help manage large datasets and complex calculations:

- **Alt + A, M**: Removes duplicates in a data set, essential for cleaning up data before analysis.
- **Ctrl + Shift + "+":** Inserts a new row or column, depending on the current selection, which is crucial when adding data to existing tables.
- **F2**: Edits the active cell, making it quick and easy to change formulas and data.
- **Ctrl + T**: Converts a data range to a table, which is highly beneficial for managing and analyzing groups of related data.

Creating Custom Shortcuts

Excel 2024 allows users to create their own custom shortcuts through macros. By recording a macro and assigning it to a custom keyboard shortcut, users can automate repetitive tasks unique to their workflow.

Steps to Create Custom Shortcuts:

1. **Record a Macro**: Go to the View tab, click Macros, and select Record Macro. Perform the task you want to automate.
2. **Stop Recording**: Once done, stop the recording and go back to the Macros menu.
3. **Assign a Shortcut**: Choose the macro, then click 'Options' and assign a shortcut key.

Custom macros can include complex sequences like formatting reports, inserting predefined formulas, or even preparing data presentations.

Integrating Shortcuts Into Daily Workflows

To fully benefit from the power of shortcuts in Excel, integrate them into your daily tasks:

- **Practice Regularly**: The more you use shortcuts, the more intuitive they become. Regular use turns these shortcuts into second nature.
- **Keep a Cheat Sheet**: Initially, keep a cheat sheet handy with your most used shortcuts until you memorize them.
- **Customize Toolbars**: For mouse users, customize the Quick Access Toolbar to include your most used commands. This isn't a keyboard shortcut but helps in reducing mouse travel time.

Mastering shortcuts in Excel 2024 is not just about learning keystrokes; it's about rethinking how you interact with software to make data handling as efficient and streamlined as possible. Whether you're a novice learning the ropes or a seasoned pro looking to shave seconds off your tasks, Excel shortcuts provide the tools necessary to enhance your productivity and data management capabilities. As you grow more proficient, you'll find that these shortcuts not only speed up your workflow but also allow for a deeper and more focused approach to data analysis. This efficiency is invaluable in a professional setting, where time saved is opportunity gained.

HIDDEN FEATURES

Excel 2024 is not just a spreadsheet application; it's a treasure trove of hidden features and shortcuts that can dramatically enhance productivity and functionality for the savvy user. Beyond the well-trodden path of common formulas and functions lies a hidden landscape brimming with lesser-known tools that cater to niche problems and specialized tasks. This sub-chapter unveils some of these hidden features, providing insights into how they can be leveraged to streamline workflows, uncover new data insights, and push the boundaries of what Excel can do for you as a professional.

Camera Tool

One of Excel's most underutilized features is the Camera tool. It allows you to take a live picture of a cell range, chart, or table, which updates dynamically if the original data changes. This tool is incredibly useful for creating dynamic dashboards where space is limited, as it allows you to place live images of important data or charts anywhere in your workbook without duplicating data.

- **How to Use**: To add the Camera tool to your Quick Access Toolbar, go to **File > Options > Quick Access Toolbar**, choose commands from **All Commands**, scroll to find the Camera, add it, and click OK. Now, select a range, click the Camera tool, and then click again in your workbook to drop a linked picture of your selected range.

XLOOKUP Function

While not exactly hidden, the XLOOKUP function is a powerful addition to Excel 2024 that many users have not yet discovered. It replaces older functions like VLOOKUP and HLOOKUP by providing a simpler, more flexible way to look up data.

- **Benefits**: XLOOKUP can return an item in an array or range of cells, and you can specify the return array, search array, and not_found behavior. It simplifies formulas by doing away with the need for multiple nested IF statements.

Power Query Editor's Advanced Features

Power Query is well-known for its data import capabilities, but many of its more advanced features are often overlooked:

- **Merging Queries**: Use Power Query to perform complex merges between data tables that go beyond simple VLOOKUPs or INDEX/MATCH combinations.
- **Conditional Columns**: Add new columns to your data, where values are based on conditions set within other columns, similar to using an IF function but more streamlined and with more powerful data processing capabilities.

Name Box Tricks

The Name Box in Excel is not just for identifying cell locations; it can be used to navigate and name ranges dynamically.

- **Named Ranges**: Instead of remembering cell references, you can name a range of cells and refer to these names in your formulas. This is especially handy for complex models.
- **Quick Navigation**: Type the name of any named range into the Name Box to instantly move to that area of your worksheet.

Using Forms for Data Entry

The often-overlooked Forms feature in Excel provides a simple way to enter data into a table without directly interacting with the spreadsheet grid. This can prevent accidental data deletion and format corruption, making it ideal for databases maintained by multiple users.

- **Accessing Forms**: You can add the Form tool to the Quick Access Toolbar from **File > Options > Quick Access Toolbar** and then select 'Forms' from the list of commands.

Advanced Conditional Formatting

Conditional Formatting is a well-known feature, but few tap into its full potential:

- **Using Formulas**: You can use formulas to determine the conditions under which cells should be formatted. This method offers limitless possibilities for visually distinguishing data based on complex criteria.
- **Highlighting Entire Rows**: Combine formulas with conditional formatting to highlight entire rows based on a single cell's value, enhancing the readability of large datasets.

The hidden features of Excel 2024 are like keys to unlock deeper functionality and more efficient data management within the application. By exploring these lesser-known tools, professionals can enhance their Excel skill set, streamline their workflows, and elevate their data analysis capabilities. Each hidden feature, whether it's a tool, function, or formatting trick, holds the potential to transform mundane data tasks into powerful insights, driving better decision-making and productivity in the workplace.

TROUBLESHOOTING EXCEL ISSUES

In the sophisticated world of Excel 2024, encountering issues can often interrupt the seamless flow of data analysis and reporting. Whether it's formulas not calculating correctly, files not opening, or data not displaying as expected, troubleshooting these issues is an essential skill for any Excel user. This sub-chapter is dedicated to exploring common Excel problems and providing systematic approaches to diagnose and resolve them, ensuring minimal disruption to your workflow and maximizing productivity.

Understanding Common Excel Issues

Excel issues typically fall into several categories, each with its unique set of challenges and solutions:

Formulas Not Working

One of the most common frustrations occurs when formulas do not work as expected. This could be due to a range of reasons from simple syntax errors to more complex issues like circular references or volatile functions causing performance lags.

- **Solution**: Check for common errors like mismatched parentheses, incorrect cell references, or accidental use of non-mathematical operators. Ensure that cell formatting is appropriate for the expected result (e.g., a cell formatted as 'text' will not properly calculate numerical formulas).

File Open or Load Issues

Problems with opening or loading Excel files can stem from file corruption, compatibility issues, or insufficient system resources.

- **Solution**: Try opening the file on a different computer or Excel version to isolate the issue. If the file is corrupted, use the 'Open and Repair' feature found under **File > Open**. Always ensure your Excel version is up to date to avoid compatibility problems.

Performance Issues

Excel's performance might lag, especially with large files, extensive formulas, or when multiple processes are running.

- **Solution**: Optimize Excel performance by minimizing the use of volatile functions like **INDIRECT** and **OFFSET**, and by converting frequently used formulas to values once their computation is no longer needed regularly. Simplify complex arrays and consider using Excel's Power Pivot feature for handling very large datasets.

Advanced Troubleshooting Techniques

For more complex issues, a deeper understanding of Excel's functionalities and settings may be required.

Data Visualization Problems

Issues with charts and graphs, such as incorrect data representation or formatting errors, can often be traced back to source data issues or misapplied settings.

- **Solution**: Double-check the data ranges selected for your charts and ensure that the correct chart type is used for your data. Use the 'Select Data Source' dialog to adjust which data is displayed and how it's processed.

Collaboration Issues

When working collaboratively on Excel files, issues such as conflicting changes or inconsistent updates can arise.

- **Solution**: Utilize Excel's built-in collaboration features like co-authoring, which provides real-time updates and conflict resolution tools. Ensure all users are operating on the same version of Excel and have appropriate access permissions set.

Advanced Error Checking

For formulas that are particularly complex or critical, Excel's error checking tool can be invaluable.

- **Solution**: Use the 'Error Checking' tool located in the 'Formulas' tab, which helps identify and debug formula errors throughout your workbook. It offers explanations for common errors and potential solutions.

Preventive Measures

To minimize troubleshooting in the future, consider implementing the following preventive measures:

- **Structured Documentation**: Maintain clear documentation of all formulas, data sources, and modifications within your workbook. This not only helps in troubleshooting but also aids others who may work on your file.
- **Regular Backups**: Set up a routine for backing up important Excel files to avoid data loss in case of software or hardware failures.
- **Continuous Learning**: Stay updated with the latest Excel features and best practices. Often, what seems like an issue can be a feature that is not fully understood.

Troubleshooting in Excel is as much about understanding what went wrong as it is about knowing the depth of Excel's features and how they can interact. By approaching Excel issues systematically, verifying data integrity, and utilizing Excel's robust set of tools for error checking and performance optimization, professionals can ensure that their use of Excel remains both productive and efficient. These strategies not only resolve immediate issues but also enhance one's overall ability to use Excel effectively, turning potential obstacles into opportunities for learning and improvement.

15. Daily Exercises: From Beginner to Pro in 24 Days

In this redesigned journey to excel in Excel 2024 over 24 days, we dive deeper and detail more specific tasks that will bolster your skills from fundamental concepts to advanced functionalities. Each day is dedicated to not only learning a feature but mastering it through practical, hands-on exercises that challenge you to apply what you've learned in real-world scenarios. Here's how each day is structured to maximize learning and retention:

Day 1: Introduction to Excel Interface

- **Objective**: Familiarize yourself with Excel's layout, focusing on understanding how to navigate efficiently.
- **Exercise**: Open Excel, identify and explore each tab on the Ribbon, especially focusing on the Home, Insert, and Data tabs. Locate and describe the functions of the Quick Access Toolbar, Formula Bar, and Status Bar.

Day 2: Creating and Formatting Worksheets

- **Objective**: Master the art of managing worksheets within a workbook.
- **Exercise**: Create a new workbook and set up three different worksheets for budget, expenses, and revenue. Customize the names and apply a unique color theme to each sheet to visually distinguish them.

Day 3: Data Entry Techniques

- **Objective**: Enhance your speed and accuracy in entering data.
- **Exercise**: Populate the 'budget' worksheet with various types of data including text (categories), numbers (figures), and dates (month, year). Implement shortcuts for data entry such as Ctrl+; for the current date.

Day 4: Basic Formulas

- **Objective**: Gain confidence in writing basic arithmetic formulas.
- **Exercise**: In your budget worksheet, use formulas to calculate the total budget, the amount spent, and the remaining balance. Use simple additions, subtractions, and multiplications.

Day 5: Working with Basic Functions

- **Objective**: Understand and apply basic functions like SUM, AVERAGE, MIN, and MAX.
- **Exercise**: Calculate the total annual budget, average monthly spending, minimum, and maximum expenses in your expenses worksheet.

Day 6: Formatting Data

- **Objective**: Learn to format data effectively to enhance readability and interpretation.
- **Exercise**: Format financial figures using currency formatting, apply conditional formatting to highlight expenses that exceed the budget, and customize the appearance of date fields.

Day 7: Introduction to Charts

- **Objective**: Start creating charts to visualize data.
- **Exercise**: Create a pie chart to represent budget allocation and a bar chart to show monthly expenses. Customize the charts by adjusting colors, labels, and legends.

Day 8: Data Sorting and Filtering

- **Objective**: Organize large datasets efficiently.
- **Exercise**: In the expenses worksheet, sort data by the amount spent and date. Apply filters to view transactions for specific categories like 'Utilities' or 'Rent'.

Day 9: Basic Data Analysis

- **Objective**: Utilize PivotTables to summarize and analyze data.
- **Exercise**: Create a PivotTable to summarize total expenses by category, using filters to switch between different months and quarters.

Day 10: Introduction to Conditional Formatting

- **Objective**: Apply conditional formatting to automate the styling based on data conditions.
- **Exercise**: Use conditional formatting in the budget worksheet to automatically highlight any categories where the spending is 75% of the budget.

Day 11: More Complex Formulas

- **Objective**: Implement more complex logical formulas using IF statements.
- **Exercise**: Add an 'Over Budget' column that uses an IF statement to show "Yes" if expenses exceed the budget and "No" otherwise.

Day 12: Using Date and Time Functions

- **Objective**: Master date and time calculations for tracking project timelines and deadlines.
- **Exercise**: Calculate the number of days until the next payment date for each expense category using the TODAY() and target date.

Day 13: Advanced Charting Techniques

- **Objective**: Explore dynamic and complex chart options.
- **Exercise**: Create a combination chart that overlays a line graph of monthly revenue over a bar chart of expenses. Adjust the secondary axis for clear visualization.

Day 14: Exploring Data Validation

- **Objective**: Implement data validation to ensure data integrity.
- **Exercise**: Set data validation rules for the expenses sheet to restrict the expense categories to a predefined list and to ensure that all entered dates are within the fiscal year.

Day 15: Advanced Use of Functions

- **Objective**: Dive into complex functions such as VLOOKUP and INDEX/MATCH.
- **Exercise**: Use VLOOKUP to find and display the budget for each category in the expenses sheet from the budget sheet.

Day 16: Introduction to Macros

- **Objective**: Discover the power of macros for automating repetitive tasks.
- **Exercise**: Record a macro that formats the expense reports, including applying borders, setting number formats, and aligning text.

Day 17: Linking Data Between Sheets

- **Objective**: Learn to integrate data across multiple worksheets.
- **Exercise**: Link the total expenses from the expenses sheet to the summary sheet to automatically update as new data is entered.

Day 18: Error Checking and Data Auditing

- **Objective**: Develop skills to identify and correct errors in data.
- **Exercise**: Use the Trace Precedents and Trace Dependents tools to identify and fix errors in the budget calculations.

Day 19: Importing and Exporting Data

- **Objective**: Manage external data effectively.
- **Exercise**: Import data from an external CSV file into the revenue sheet and export the summary sheet as a PDF for sharing with stakeholders.

Day 20: Advanced Data Management

- **Objective**: Consolidate data from multiple sources for comprehensive analysis.
- **Exercise**: Use 3D references to consolidate monthly data into a yearly overview sheet.

Day 21: Custom Views and Reporting

- **Objective**: Customize the viewing options to streamline reporting processes.
- **Exercise**: Set up custom views in Excel to quickly switch between different types of data analysis without rearranging your data manually.

Day 22: Advanced Conditional Formatting

- **Objective**: Apply complex rules for conditional formatting to provide deeper insights into data trends.
- **Exercise**: Use a formula to apply formatting that highlights rows in the expense report where the spend is more than 10% over budget.

Day 23: Optimizing Workbook Performance

- **Objective**: Enhance the performance of your Excel workbook.
- **Exercise**: Optimize the workbook by converting frequently updated formulas to static values, reducing the size of the workbook, and removing unused elements.

Day 24: Final Project

- **Objective**: Combine all learned Excel functions and features to create a comprehensive, interactive financial dashboard.
- **Exercise**: Design a dashboard that includes slicers for selecting different time periods, charts that update based on selected data, and dynamic tables that reflect current financial statuses.

By the end of this structured 24-day program, you'll have developed not only proficiency in Excel's core and advanced features but also an integrated approach to using these tools in synergy to manage and analyze data effectively. This hands-on practice ensures that you are equipped to tackle any Excel challenge and turn raw data into actionable insights.

REAL-WORLD SCENARIOS

The true test of any skill lies in its application to real-world scenarios. For Excel users, the leap from theoretical exercises to practical, everyday applications marks a significant milestone. This sub-chapter guides you through a series of real-world scenarios that mirror the challenges and tasks you might encounter in a professional setting. Each scenario is designed to consolidate your learning from the previous exercises and apply these skills in a holistic and practical manner.

Scenario 1: Annual Budget Planning

Background: You are a financial analyst at a mid-sized corporation tasked with creating the annual budget for the upcoming fiscal year. The budget needs to be broken down by department and must include projections based on historical spending data.

Tasks:

1. **Data Compilation**: Consolidate past years' spending data from various departmental reports into a single Excel workbook.
2. **Analysis**: Use PivotTables to analyze spending trends and predict the next year's budget.
3. **Presentation**: Create a dashboard that includes charts and tables, providing a clear visual representation of the budget for presentation to senior management.

Skills Applied: Data import, PivotTables, chart creation, dashboard design.

Scenario 2: Sales Performance Tracking

Background: You work in sales management and need to track the performance of 20 sales representatives across several regions, comparing their sales figures against set targets.

Tasks:

1. **Data Setup**: Enter monthly sales data and targets into Excel.
2. **Performance Calculation**: Use formulas to calculate each sales representative's performance against targets.
3. **Reporting**: Generate a report using Conditional Formatting to highlight areas where sales targets have not been met and create a line chart to display trends over time.

Skills Applied: Formula use, Conditional Formatting, chart creation.

Scenario 3: Inventory Management

Background: As the inventory manager for a retail business, you need to maintain an up-to-date inventory list that tracks stock levels, reordering statuses, and supplier information.

Tasks:

1. **Inventory Listing**: Create a comprehensive list of inventory items with current stock levels, reorder levels, and supplier details.
2. **Reorder Status**: Use logical functions to determine which items need reordering based on minimum stock levels.
3. **Supplier Contact**: Link each item with suppliers' contact information for quick access.

Skills Applied: Data entry, logical functions (IF, AND), linking data.

Scenario 4: Customer Feedback Analysis

Background: You are responsible for analyzing customer feedback to identify areas of improvement. The feedback is collected via surveys and stored in an Excel file.

Tasks:

1. **Data Cleaning**: Organize and clean the data collected from various sources to prepare it for analysis.
2. **Sentiment Analysis**: Categorize feedback into positive, negative, and neutral using text functions.
3. **Summary Report**: Create a report summarizing the key findings with appropriate charts to illustrate customer satisfaction trends.

Skills Applied: Data cleaning, text functions, report generation, chart creation.

Scenario 5: Project Scheduling and Tracking

Background: You are a project manager needing to create a detailed project schedule that tracks task progress against deadlines.

Tasks:

1. **Schedule Setup**: Use Excel to create a Gantt chart-like schedule that includes start and end dates for each task.
2. **Progress Tracking**: Implement a system within the schedule to update task progress and highlight any delays using Conditional Formatting.
3. **Resource Allocation**: Develop a resource allocation table that shows which resources are assigned to specific tasks.

Skills Applied: Date functions, Conditional Formatting, creating and using tables.

Scenario 6: Financial Reporting for Tax Purposes

Background: It's the end of the fiscal year, and you need to prepare detailed financial reports for tax filing, which involves summarizing incomes, expenses, and deductions.

Tasks:

1. **Data Summarization**: Use advanced formulas to calculate total income, expenses, and potential deductions.
2. **Tax Calculation**: Apply tax rates to compute payable taxes.
3. **Report Creation**: Design a comprehensive financial report that can be submitted to the tax authorities.

Skills Applied: Advanced formulas, financial calculations, professional report formatting.

Each of these scenarios not only tests your ability to navigate Excel's features but also encourages you to think critically about how these tools can be used to solve practical problems. By engaging with these real-world challenges, you refine your skills, readying yourself for any task that might arise in your professional journey with Excel.

PROGRESS TRACKING

Embarking on a structured learning journey requires not only dedication and focus but also a methodical way to track your progress. In the realm of mastering Excel, progress tracking is crucial because it not only measures growth but also illuminates areas that need more attention or different strategies. This sub-chapter discusses how you can effectively monitor your advancement through the 24-day Excel training program, using Excel itself as your primary tool for tracking and assessment.

Designing Your Progress Tracker in Excel

To effectively monitor your journey from beginner to pro, you'll create a dynamic progress tracking system within Excel. This tracker will serve not just as a record of completed tasks but also as a dashboard that provides visual feedback on your mastery of various Excel functions and concepts.

Setting Up the Tracker

1. **Structure**: Start by setting up a table in Excel where each row represents a day in the program, and the columns include details such as the date, the core focus of the day, objectives met, time spent, and a self-assessment score.

2. **Dropdown Lists**: Utilize dropdown lists to standardize entries for consistency and ease of analysis. For example, you might include dropdown options for 'Objectives Met' like 'Fully', 'Partially', or 'Not Met'.

3. **Time Tracking**: Implement a simple time tracking by entering the start and end times of each session, using Excel to calculate the total duration spent each day. This helps in understanding the time investment and can be critical for managing your learning pace.

Incorporating Formulas and Functions

- **Conditional Formatting**: Use conditional formatting to visually signify progress. For example, cells under 'Objectives Met' can change color based on the status: green for 'Fully', yellow for 'Partially', and red for 'Not Met'.

- **Automated Summaries**: Summarize data with formulas to calculate total hours spent, average daily learning time, and average self-assessment score. This summary provides quick insights into your dedication and progress.

- **Graphical Analysis**: Create charts to visually track your progress over time. Line graphs or bar charts can illustrate how much time you've spent or how your self-assessment scores have improved, making it easier to spot trends and assess effectiveness.

Daily Entries and Reflections

As part of your daily routine, enter the specifics of each day's activities into the tracker. Include what exercises were done, which areas were challenging, and how well the day's objectives were met. This not only records your activity but also encourages reflection, a critical component of effective learning.

- **Objective Alignment**: Reflect on whether the day's learning aligned with the set objectives and how these contribute to your overall Excel mastery. This reflection helps in connecting daily activities with broader learning goals.
- **Challenges Faced**: Note any specific challenges you encountered. This can be instrumental for revisiting difficult concepts or for seeking additional resources to overcome these hurdles.
- **Self-Assessment**: Rate your performance or understanding daily using a simple scale (e.g., 1-5). This self-assessment helps in identifying days or areas where you might need to invest more effort or seek additional help.

Weekly Reviews and Adjustments

At the end of each week, take a deeper dive into your tracker's data to evaluate your weekly performance. This review is crucial for adjusting your learning plan to better suit your needs or to spend extra time on concepts that aren't sticking as well as others.

- **Performance Trends**: Analyze trends from your weekly data to identify any continuous difficulties or strong points in your learning curve.
- **Plan Adjustments**: Based on your review, adjust your upcoming learning plans. For example, if you find PivotTables particularly challenging, you might decide to allocate more time to that topic in the following days.
- **Resource Enhancement**: Seek additional resources like tutorials, forums, or peer help based on the areas highlighted during your weekly reviews.

Effective progress tracking in Excel is not just about keeping a log of completed tasks; it's about creating a feedback loop that enhances your learning through constant monitoring and adjustments. By utilizing Excel's capabilities to track, assess, and visualize your progress, you turn the tool you're mastering into an ally in your learning journey. This meta-use of Excel not only reinforces your skills but also deepens your understanding of its application in real-world scenarios. Through meticulous tracking and thoughtful reflection, you ensure that each step taken is solid, measurable, and contributes significantly to your goal of becoming proficient in Excel.

16. THE 15-DAY EXCEL CHALLENGE

In the landscape of business analytics, the ability to efficiently analyze a sales report can significantly impact strategic decision-making. The following test exercise, designed as part of our 15-Day Excel Challenge, focuses on harnessing Excel 2024 to perform a comprehensive sales report analysis. This exercise is crafted to test your skills in data manipulation, analysis, and presentation, reflecting typical challenges faced by professionals in real-world scenarios.

Context and Objective

You are provided with a dataset containing sales information for a multi-national corporation for the fiscal year 2024. This dataset includes details such as product ID, category, region, salesperson, number of units sold, unit price, and date of sale. Your task is to analyze this data to identify trends, assess sales performance, and provide actionable insights.

Dataset Overview

The dataset includes the following columns:
- **Product ID**: Unique identifier for each product.
- **Category**: Product category (e.g., Electronics, Apparel, Home Appliances).
- **Region**: Geographic region of the sale (e.g., North America, Europe, Asia).
- **Salesperson**: Name of the salesperson who made the sale.
- **Units Sold**: Number of units sold in each transaction.
- **Unit Price**: Price per unit.
- **Date of Sale**: Date on which the sale was made.

Tasks

Task 1: Data Cleaning and Preparation
- **Objective**: Prepare your dataset for analysis by cleaning and structuring the data.
- **Actions**:
  - Check for and handle missing values in the dataset.
  - Ensure all data types are correct (e.g., dates are recognized as dates).
  - Create a new column for total sales value (Units Sold * Unit Price).

Task 2: Data Analysis

- **Objective**: Perform a thorough analysis to extract meaningful insights from the sales data.
- **Actions**:
  - Generate a summary report showing total sales by region and category.
  - Use PivotTables to analyze the data from multiple angles, such as total sales per salesperson and category-wise sales per region.
  - Identify the top 5 best-selling products across different regions.

Task 3: Trend Analysis

- **Objective**: Analyze trends over the months and provide observations.
- **Actions**:
  - Create a line chart to visualize monthly sales trends.
  - Analyze seasonal patterns and sales performance trends throughout the year.

Task 4: Advanced Analysis

- **Objective**: Delve deeper into the data to uncover underlying patterns.
- **Actions**:
  - Conduct a cohort analysis to see how sales patterns differ by product launch year.
  - Use conditional formatting to highlight regions and categories that are performing above or below average.

Task 5: Report and Presentation

- **Objective**: Develop a comprehensive report summarizing your findings with charts and insights.
- **Actions**:
  - Create a dashboard summarizing key metrics, including total sales, average sale per unit, and sales by category and region.
  - Prepare a presentation slide deck summarizing the analytical insights, suitable for a management review.

Deliverables

- **Excel Workbook**: Contains the cleaned data, analysis, and charts.
- **Excel Dashboard**: A dynamic dashboard highlighting key sales metrics and trends.
- **Presentation**: A PowerPoint presentation outlining key findings and business insights.

Evaluation Criteria

- **Accuracy**: Correctness of the data cleaning process, calculations, and analysis.
- **Insightfulness**: Depth and relevance of the insights generated from the data.
- **Presentation**: Effectiveness in communicating findings through the dashboard and presentation slides.
- **Creativity**: Innovative approaches in analysis and visualization.

This exercise challenges you to apply your Excel skills in a scenario that mimics a real-life business analysis task, focusing on extracting actionable insights from complex data. It tests a range of competencies from basic data handling to advanced analytical and presentation skills, preparing you for data-driven decision-making roles. By the end of this exercise, you should be able to demonstrate not just proficiency in Excel's technical capabilities, but also an ability to think critically about data and how it can inform business strategy.

TEST EXERCISE 2: INVENTORY MANAGEMENT

In the realm of supply chain management, maintaining an efficient and accurate inventory system is crucial for the health and operation of any business. This test exercise, designed for Day 2 of our 15-Day Excel Challenge, focuses on applying Excel 2024 to manage and analyze inventory effectively. This scenario will challenge your ability to use Excel for inventory tracking, forecasting, and reporting, crucial skills in logistics and operations management.

Scenario Overview

You are the inventory manager for a regional distributor that handles a diverse range of products. Your primary responsibility is to manage inventory levels, ensure adequate stock is available to meet customer demand without overstocking, and generate reports for the upper management.

Data Provided

You are provided with an initial dataset containing the following information:

- **Product ID**: Unique identifier for each product.
- **Product Name**: Name of the product.
- **Category**: The category of the product (e.g., Electronics, Apparel, Kitchenware).
- **Current Stock**: The number of units currently in the warehouse.
- **Reorder Level**: The stock level at which a new order should be placed.
- **Lead Time**: The number of days it takes from ordering a product to its delivery.
- **Yearly Sales**: Units sold per year.

Tasks

Task 1: Inventory Status Update

- **Objective**: Update the inventory status by identifying items that need reordering.
- **Actions**:
  - Calculate the 'Order Needed' status for each product by comparing the current stock with the reorder level.
  - Use a formula to determine which items fall below the reorder threshold and mark them as 'Order Now'.

Task 2: Forecasting Future Inventory Needs

- **Objective**: Forecast inventory needs based on sales trends and lead time.
- **Actions**:
  - Calculate the projected end-of-month stock levels using current stock and average monthly sales (derived from yearly sales).
  - Adjust the forecast based on lead time, ensuring that orders are placed in time to replenish stock before it dips below critical levels.

Task 3: Optimization of Stock Levels

- **Objective**: Optimize stock levels to ensure efficient inventory turnover.
- **Actions**:
  - Identify overstocked items by comparing current stock to average sales and adjust reorder levels accordingly.
  - Use conditional formatting to highlight items that are significantly over or under the ideal stock level.

Task 4: Automated Ordering System

- **Objective**: Create an automated system to suggest order quantities.
- **Actions**:
  - Develop a formula to suggest order quantities based on the reorder level, current stock, and lead time.
  - Integrate a simple 'Order' button using Excel macros that simulates placing an order for understocked items.

Task 5: Reporting for Management

- **Objective**: Prepare a monthly inventory report for management.
- **Actions**:
    - Create a comprehensive report that includes current stock, order status, and forecasted needs.
    - Design a dashboard that visually represents the inventory data, using PivotTables and charts to summarize the inventory status, highlight critical shortages or overstocks, and display trends in order replenishment.

Deliverables

- **Excel Workbook**: Contains the updated inventory list, formulas for forecasting, and the automated ordering system.
- **Inventory Dashboard**: A dynamic Excel dashboard that provides real-time insights into inventory levels, order status, and stock forecasts.
- **Monthly Report**: A detailed report that outlines inventory status, identifies potential issues, and provides actionable recommendations.

Evaluation Criteria

- **Accuracy**: Precision in formulas and calculations used for forecasting and reporting.
- **Innovation**: Creativity in developing the automated ordering system and optimizing inventory management processes.
- **Clarity**: Effectiveness of the dashboard and report in communicating key inventory metrics to management.
- **Practicality**: Relevance and applicability of the suggested order quantities and inventory adjustments to real-world operations.

This exercise is designed to test and enhance your proficiency with Excel in handling complex, dynamic inventory management tasks. By successfully completing this challenge, you will demonstrate not only technical expertise in Excel but also a strategic understanding of inventory control, crucial for any role in operations management. Through this hands-on scenario, you'll gain valuable insights into the practical challenges of inventory management and develop robust tools to address these challenges efficiently.

TEST EXERCISE 3-15: VARIOUS DATA PROJECTS

The final segment of the 15-Day Excel Challenge is designed to comprehensively evaluate and expand your Excel expertise through a series of 13 varied data projects. Each project is tailored to challenge different aspects of Excel—from data analysis and visual reporting to financial modeling and decision support systems. These projects will not only consolidate your existing knowledge but also push the boundaries of your capabilities in using Excel for complex, real-world business scenarios.

Project Overview

Each of the following projects is structured to simulate typical challenges faced in a business environment, requiring a combination of Excel skills to effectively address them.

Test Exercise 3: Customer Segmentation Analysis

- **Objective**: Analyze customer data to identify distinct segments based on purchasing behavior.
- **Tasks**: Use clustering techniques through Excel's data analysis toolpak to classify customers. Visualize the segmentation with scatter plots and provide strategic recommendations for marketing.

Test Exercise 4: Financial Forecasting Model

- **Objective**: Develop a financial forecasting model for a startup's next fiscal year.
- **Tasks**: Create a model using historical sales data, predict future revenues using linear regression, and assess financial health through projected cash flows.

Test Exercise 5: Dynamic Pricing Tool

- **Objective**: Construct a tool to adjust product pricing in real-time based on market demand.
- **Tasks**: Utilize Excel's advanced formulas to simulate demand elasticity and incorporate external data feeds to adjust prices dynamically.

Test Exercise 6: Project Portfolio Management

- **Objective**: Develop a system for managing a portfolio of projects, including timelines, resources, and budgets.
- **Tasks**: Create a dashboard that tracks project status, resource allocation, and budget expenditures, with conditional formatting to highlight deviations from the plan.

Test Exercise 7: Human Resources Analytics

- **Objective**: Analyze employee data to understand turnover rates and predict future hiring needs.
- **Tasks**: Calculate turnover rates, use logistic regression to predict potential future exits, and create a plan for future hiring.

Test Exercise 8: Supply Chain Optimization

- **Objective**: Optimize the supply chain by analyzing vendor performance and logistics costs.
- **Tasks**: Assess vendor reliability and cost-effectiveness using scorecards, and model logistics scenarios to minimize costs.

Test Exercise 9: Risk Management Framework

- **Objective**: Implement a risk management framework to identify and mitigate business risks.
- **Tasks**: Develop a risk matrix based on likelihood and impact. Use Excel's scenario analysis feature to simulate different risk scenarios and their mitigation strategies.

Test Exercise 10: Marketing ROI Analysis

- **Objective**: Evaluate the return on investment (ROI) for various marketing campaigns.
- **Tasks**: Analyze campaign data to calculate ROI, visualize results with charts, and suggest reallocations of budget based on performance.

Test Exercise 11: Compliance Tracking System

- **Objective**: Create a compliance tracking system for regulatory requirements.
- **Tasks**: Design a system that tracks compliance status across multiple departments, highlighting areas of concern and upcoming deadlines.

Test Exercise 12: Inventory Replenishment Model
- **Objective**: Build a model that forecasts inventory needs and schedules replenishments.
- **Tasks**: Integrate sales forecasts with stock levels to create a dynamic ordering system that updates automatically as sales data is received.

Test Exercise 13: Customer Service Dashboard
- **Objective**: Design a dashboard that provides insights into customer service performance.
- **Tasks**: Compile customer service data into a comprehensive dashboard, showcasing response times, satisfaction ratings, and areas for improvement.

Test Exercise 14: Business Expansion Analysis
- **Objective**: Analyze potential business expansion scenarios to determine the most viable option.
- **Tasks**: Model different expansion scenarios using Excel's financial functions and create a decision matrix for evaluation.

Test Exercise 15: Sustainability Impact Report
- **Objective**: Prepare a report analyzing the sustainability impacts of a company's operations.
- **Tasks**: Aggregate data on energy consumption, waste management, and recycling activities to evaluate environmental impact and prepare a report detailing findings and recommendations.

Deliverables for Each Project
- **Excel Workbook**: Contains all data analyses, models, and tools developed.
- **Visual Summary**: A dashboard or a set of charts/graphs summarizing key insights and outcomes from each project.
- **Executive Summary**: A brief report accompanying each project that outlines the approach, findings, and strategic recommendations.

These exercises are designed to challenge you to apply a broad range of Excel functionalities to solve complex problems. Completing these will not only deepen your understanding of Excel's capabilities but also enhance your problem-solving skills in a professional context. Each project completed adds to your portfolio, showcasing your ability to leverage Excel as a powerful tool for business intelligence.

APPENDICES

EXCEL FUNCTION DICTIONARY

Welcome to the Excel Function Dictionary, a comprehensive guide designed to help you navigate through the extensive list of functions available in Excel 2024. This dictionary is crafted not merely as a reference tool, but as a bridge to deeper understanding and application of Excel's powerful functions for data analysis, financial calculations, text manipulation, and beyond. Here, each function is unpacked with its syntax, uses, and practical examples, enhancing your fluency in Excel and empowering you to handle complex tasks with ease.

1. SUM Function

- **Purpose**: Adds all the numbers in a range of cells.
- **Syntax**: **SUM(number1, [number2], ...)**
- **Example**: If **A1:A5** contains numbers 10, 20, 30, 40, and 50, then **SUM(A1:A5)** returns 150.

2. AVERAGE Function

- **Purpose**: Calculates the average of the numbers in a range of cells.
- **Syntax**: **AVERAGE(number1, [number2], ...)**
- **Example**: For the same range **A1:A5**, **AVERAGE(A1:A5)** returns 30.

3. VLOOKUP Function

- **Purpose**: Searches for a value in the first column of a table, and returns a value in the same row from a specified column.
- **Syntax**: **VLOOKUP(lookup_value, table_array, col_index_num, [range_lookup])**
- **Example**: **VLOOKUP("Apple", A1:B5, 2, FALSE)** searches for "Apple" in the first column of **A1:B5** and returns the value from the second column.

4. IF Function

- **Purpose**: Performs a logical test and returns one value for a TRUE result, and another for a FALSE result.
- **Syntax: IF(logical_test, value_if_true, [value_if_false])**
- **Example: IF(A1 > 10, "Over 10", "10 or less")** checks if **A1** is greater than 10 and returns "Over 10" if true, or "10 or less" if false.

5. CONCATENATE Function

- **Purpose**: Joins two or more text strings into one string.
- **Syntax: CONCATENATE(text1, [text2], ...)**
- **Example: CONCATENATE("Hello ", "World")** returns "Hello World".

6. XLOOKUP Function

- **Purpose**: Searches a range or an array, and returns an item corresponding to the first match it finds.
- **Syntax: XLOOKUP(lookup_value, lookup_array, return_array, [if_not_found], [match_mode], [search_mode])**
- **Example: XLOOKUP("Apple", A1:A5, B1:B5)** would find "Apple" in **A1:A5** and return the corresponding value from **B1:B5**.

7. INDEX Function

- **Purpose**: Returns the value of a cell in a table based on the column and row number.
- **Syntax: INDEX(array, row_num, [column_num])**
- **Example: INDEX(A1:C3, 2, 3)** returns the value in the second row and third column of the range **A1:C3**.

8. MATCH Function

- **Purpose**: Searches for a specified item in a range of cells, and returns the relative position of that item.
- **Syntax: MATCH(lookup_value, lookup_array, [match_type])**
- **Example: MATCH("find me", A1:A5, 0)** searches for "find me" in the range **A1:A5** and returns its position.

9. COUNTIF Function

- **Purpose**: Counts the number of cells within a range that meet a single criterion.
- **Syntax**: COUNTIF(range, criteria)
- **Example**: COUNTIF(A1:A5, ">20") counts the number of cells in **A1:A5** that contain numbers greater than 20.

10. SUMIF Function

- **Purpose**: Adds the cells specified by a given condition or criteria.
- **Syntax**: SUMIF(range, criteria, [sum_range])
- **Example**: SUMIF(A1:A5, ">20", B1:B5) adds all the numbers in the range **B1:B5** where the corresponding cells in the range **A1:A5** fulfill the condition ">20".

11. COUNTA Function

- **Purpose**: Counts the number of cells that are not empty in a range.
- **Syntax**: COUNTA(value1, [value2], ...)
- **Example**: COUNTA(A1:A10) returns the number of non-empty cells in the range A1 to A10.

12. OFFSET Function

- **Purpose**: Returns a reference offset from a given starting cell or range of cells along a particular number of rows and columns.
- **Syntax**: OFFSET(reference, rows, cols, [height], [width])
- **Example**: OFFSET(A1, 3, 2) returns the cell that is three rows down and two columns to the right of cell A1.

13. INDIRECT Function

- **Purpose**: Returns a reference specified by a text string. This is useful when you want to change the reference to a cell within a formula without changing the formula itself.
- **Syntax**: INDIRECT(ref_text, [a1])
- **Example**: INDIRECT("A" & 1) returns the value in A1.

14. ROUND Function

- **Purpose**: Rounds a number to a specified number of digits.
- **Syntax: ROUND(number, num_digits)**
- **Example: ROUND(3.14159, 2)** returns 3.14.

15. MOD Function

- **Purpose**: Returns the remainder after a number is divided by a divisor. It's useful in formulas to determine even or odd results and in creating patterns.
- **Syntax: MOD(number, divisor)**
- **Example: MOD(10, 3)** returns 1, as 10 divided by 3 leaves a remainder of 1.

16. TEXT Function

- **Purpose**: Converts a value to text in a specified number format.
- **Syntax: TEXT(value, format_text)**
- **Example: TEXT(1234.567, "$#,##0.00")** converts 1234.567 to "$1,234.57".

17. NOW Function

- **Purpose**: Returns the current date and time.
- **Syntax: NOW()**
- **Example: NOW()** returns the current system date and time.

18. DATE Function

- **Purpose**: Returns the number that represents the date in Microsoft Excel date-time code.
- **Syntax: DATE(year, month, day)**
- **Example: DATE(2020, 12, 31)** returns the serial number of December 31, 2020.

19. NETWORKDAYS Function

- **Purpose**: Returns the number of whole working days between two dates.
- **Syntax: NETWORKDAYS(start_date, end_date, [holidays])**
- **Example: NETWORKDAYS(DATE(2024, 1, 1), DATE(2024, 1, 31))** calculates the number of working days in January 2024, excluding weekends.

20. HLOOKUP Function

- **Purpose**: Searches for a value in the top row of a table or an array of values, and then returns a value in the same column from a row you specify in the table or array.
- **Syntax**: HLOOKUP(lookup_value, table_array, row_index_num, [range_lookup])
- **Example**: HLOOKUP("Total", A1:D4, 4, FALSE) searches for the value "Total" in the first row of A1:D4 and returns the value from the fourth row in the same column.

21. NPV Function

- **Purpose**: Calculates the net present value of an investment based on a series of periodic cash flows and a discount rate.
- **Syntax**: NPV(rate, value1, [value2], ...)
- **Example**: NPV(0.1, -10000, 3000, 4200, 6800) calculates the net present value of an investment with an initial outlay of $10,000 and cash inflows of $3,000, $4,200, and $6,800 over three periods at a discount rate of 10%.

22. IRR Function

- **Purpose**: Returns the internal rate of return for a series of cash flows represented by the numbers in a list.
- **Syntax**: IRR(values, [guess])
- **Example**: IRR(A1:A4) would calculate the internal rate of return for cash flows listed in cells A1 through A4.

23. PMT Function

- **Purpose**: Calculates the payment for a loan based on constant payments and a constant interest rate.
- **Syntax**: PMT(rate, nper, pv, [fv], [type])
- **Example**: PMT(0.05/12, 60, -5000) calculates the monthly payment for a $5,000 loan at an annual interest rate of 5% over 5 years.

24. FREQUENCY Function

- **Purpose**: Calculates how often values occur within a range of values, and returns a vertical array of numbers. It is especially useful for creating histogram data for a frequency distribution.
- **Syntax**: FREQUENCY(data_array, bins_array)
- **Example**: Suppose **A1:A10** contains numbers and **B1:B3** contains bin thresholds. **FREQUENCY(A1:A10, B1:B3)** returns a vertical array with counts of values in each bin.

25. TRANSPOSE Function

- **Purpose**: Returns a vertical range of cells as a horizontal range, or vice versa. This function is essential when you need to switch the orientation of a rectangular array or range without manually rearranging the data.
- **Syntax**: TRANSPOSE(array)
- **Example**: **TRANSPOSE(A1:C3)** would switch a 3x3 matrix from horizontal to vertical or vice versa.

Each function listed in this dictionary is a building block that, when combined with others, can solve virtually any data-related challenge you encounter in Excel. Whether you're making financial models, analyzing scientific data, or managing a database, understanding these functions and their applications will enable you to harness the full power of Excel effectively and efficiently. This dictionary serves not only as a guide to learning individual functions but also as a springboard for innovative problem-solving and sophisticated data analysis.

EXCEL ERROR TYPES AND SOLUTIONS

Encountering errors in Excel is not just a test of your problem-solving skills; it's an opportunity to deepen your understanding of how Excel operates under the hood. This sub-chapter delves into common Excel error types and their solutions, equipping you with the knowledge to swiftly diagnose and rectify issues that may arise during your data analysis tasks. Understanding these errors will enhance your efficiency and accuracy in handling data within Excel.

Common Excel Errors and How to Fix Them

#DIV/0! Error

- **What It Means**: This error appears when a formula attempts to divide a number by zero or an empty cell.
- **Example**: **=A1/B1** will display #DIV/0! if B1 contains 0.
- **Solution**: Use the **IFERROR** function to catch and handle this error. Example: **=IFERROR(A1/B1, "Error in calculation")** would return "Error in calculation" instead of #DIV/0!.

#VALUE! Error

- **What It Means**: This error is shown when the wrong type of argument or operand is used. It frequently occurs when functions like **SUM** or **AVERAGE** receive non-numeric data.
- **Example**: **=SUM("Ten", 20)** results in #VALUE! because "Ten" is not a number.
- **Solution**: Ensure that all inputs are valid numerical values. Use the **VALUE** function if necessary to convert text that represents numbers into numbers: **=SUM(VALUE("10"), 20)**.

#REF! Error

- **What It Means**: This error signifies a reference issue where a formula contains an invalid cell reference. This often happens after deleting a row, column, or cell that was part of a formula.
- **Example**: If cell A1 contains a reference to B1 (**=B1**), and B1 is deleted, A1 will show #REF!.
- **Solution**: Check the formula for cell references that no longer exist and adjust them accordingly. Utilize named ranges to minimize this risk.

#NAME? Error

- **What It Means**: This occurs when Excel doesn't recognize text in a formula. Often, this is due to misspelling a function name or referencing a named range that doesn't exist.
- **Example**: **=SUMX(A1:A10)** will result in #NAME? since there is no function **SUMX**.
- **Solution**: Verify that all function names and named ranges are spelled correctly. Use the **Formula** tab to insert functions to avoid typos.

#N/A Error

- **What It Means**: Represents "Not Available" and is commonly seen when a function like **VLOOKUP** cannot find a reference result in the source it's searching.
- **Example**: =VLOOKUP("apple", A2:B10, 2, FALSE) displays #N/A if "apple" is not in the first column of the range A2:B10.
- **Solution**: Ensure the lookup value exists in the source range. Consider alternative or additional data cleansing or preparation steps to ensure alignment between data sources.

#NUM! Error

- **What It Means**: Indicates a numerical error when a formula or function contains invalid numeric values for the operation it is performing.
- **Example**: =SQRT(-1) triggers #NUM! because the square root of a negative number is not defined.
- **Solution**: Check the numeric values in your formulas to ensure they are within a valid range for the specific operations being performed.

#GETTING_DATA Error

- **What It Means**: This is a placeholder error that appears temporarily when Excel is in the process of retrieving external data or when performing calculations that require data from an external source.
- **Example**: When pulling data from an SQL server or a web query, Excel might momentarily display #GETTING_DATA.
- **Solution**: This error typically resolves on its own once Excel completes the data retrieval process. If it persists, check the data connection and ensure the external data source is accessible and functioning correctly.

#SPILL! Error

- **What It Means**: Occurs when a formula that generates multiple results (an array formula) cannot deliver a result because neighboring cells contain data.
- **Example**: If **A1** has the formula **=SEQUENCE(3)** and cells **A2** or **A3** are not empty, Excel will show #SPILL! in **A1**.
- **Solution**: Clear or move the contents from the cells that are obstructing the spill range of the formula. Alternatively, you can select another area of your worksheet that is free from such obstructions.

#CALC! Error

- **What It Means**: Indicates an issue with calculating a formula, often due to a problem with custom functions or a malfunction within Excel's calculation engine.
- **Example**: This error might occur when a custom function in VBA fails to execute due to programming errors or data type mismatches.
- **Solution**: Review the custom function code for errors. Ensure that all variables and data types are appropriately handled. Restarting Excel can also sometimes resolve calculation issues if the problem is related to the program's state.

#FIELD! Error

- **What It Means**: This error is typically associated with PivotTables or data retrieval functions where a specified field is invalid or not present in the source data.
- **Example**: If you attempt to retrieve data using **=GETPIVOTDATA("Sales", $A$1, "Product", "Bike")** and there is no "Product" field in the PivotTable, Excel will return #FIELD!.
- **Solution**: Verify that all field names are correctly spelled and that they correspond accurately to those in the source data or PivotTable. Check that your data range or data model includes all the fields your formulas are attempting to access.

#UNKNOWN! Error

- **What It Means**: This is a less common error and occurs when Excel cannot recognize a function or command. It could be due to several issues including version compatibility or corruption within the workbook.
- **Example**: Using a newer function from Excel 2024 in an earlier version of Excel might result in this error, as the older version does not recognize the function.
- **Solution**: Ensure that all users are operating on the version of Excel that supports all used functions. If the error occurs unexpectedly, consider repairing the Excel installation, or check the workbook for corruption and restore it from a backup if necessary.

Streamlining Error Handling in Excel

Adopting best practices for error handling in Excel can greatly reduce the frequency and impact of errors:

- **Consistent Data Verification**: Regularly check your data inputs and formulas for accuracy and consistency to prevent errors from arising.

- **Use of Error Handling Functions**: Incorporate functions like **IFERROR** and **IFNA** in your formulas to manage how Excel handles errors when they occur, providing alternative results or meaningful messages instead of default error codes.
- **Regular Training and Updates**: Keep up-to-date with the latest Excel features and updates. Training sessions can help users learn how to avoid common mistakes that lead to errors.

By understanding these additional error types and their solutions, you can further enhance your proficiency in Excel, ensuring that your work remains not only productive but also robust against the common pitfalls of spreadsheet management. This knowledge empowers you to tackle complex datasets and analytical tasks with confidence, ensuring that your results are both accurate and reliable.

Circular Reference Warning

- **What It Means**: A circular reference occurs when a formula refers to its own cell, either directly or through a chain of references involving other cells.
- **Example**: If A1 contains **=A1+1**, this creates a circular reference.
- **Solution**: Modify the formula to remove the self-reference. If circular references are intentional for iterative calculations, enable iterative calculations via File > Options > Formulas, and set the maximum iterations and tolerance levels accordingly.

Advanced Troubleshooting Tips

- **Using Formula Auditing Tools**: Excel's formula auditing tools can help identify and correct errors in formulas. The Trace Precedents and Trace Dependents features are particularly useful for understanding how formulas are interconnected.
- **Error Checking**: Use the **Error Checking** feature under the Formulas tab to step through each error found in a worksheet. This tool offers explanations and potential fixes for common problems.

By mastering these error resolutions, you transform potential stumbling blocks into stepping stones towards proficiency. The skills to troubleshoot and resolve issues not only make your workflow smoother but also significantly enhance your credibility and capability as an Excel expert. This proactive approach to understanding and addressing Excel errors ensures that your data analysis is both robust and reliable, paving the way for insightful, error-free reporting.

In the quest to master Excel and transform it into a powerful tool for data analysis, visualization, and decision-making, the journey does not end with this guide alone. Beyond the chapters of this book, a wealth of resources awaits those eager to deepen their understanding and refine their skills. This sub-chapter is dedicated to guiding you towards further reading and resources that will continue your education in Excel, broadening your capabilities and enhancing your insight into this indispensable tool.

Books on Advanced Excel Techniques

1. **"Excel Bible" by John Walkenbach**
   - Known as "Mr. Spreadsheet," Walkenbach has written arguably the most comprehensive guide to Excel available. The book covers everything from basic introductions to advanced features, making it an essential addition to any Excel user's library.

2. **"Power Pivot and Power BI: The Excel User's Guide" by Rob Collie & Avichal Singh**
   - This book introduces Power Pivot and Power BI, two of Excel's most powerful data analysis tools. It's written in an accessible style that brings complex concepts down to a level that is understandable for all users.

3. **"Excel Dashboards and Reports" by Michael Alexander**
   - For those looking to transform raw data into digestible and visually engaging reports, Alexander's book provides step-by-step tutorials and practical examples on creating top-notch dashboards and reports.

Online Courses and Tutorials

1. **LinkedIn Learning (Formerly Lynda.com)**
   - Offering a range of tutorials from beginner to advanced levels, LinkedIn Learning is a treasure trove for those looking to step-by-step instructions on various Excel functions and features.

2. **Coursera and Udemy**
   - These platforms offer courses like "Excel Skills for Business" and "Microsoft Excel - Excel from Beginner to Advanced," which cater to learners at different stages of their Excel journey.

3. **Microsoft's Excel Training Center**
   - Microsoft offers free training guides, how-to articles, templates, and videos that cover new features and basic functions of Excel. These resources are excellent for staying updated with the latest additions to Excel.

Blogs and Online Forums

1. **Chandoo.org**
   - A comprehensive blog that includes tutorials, downloadable templates, and forums where users can ask questions and share knowledge about Excel. It's particularly good for those looking to hone their dashboard and visualization skills.

2. **MrExcel.com**
   - This online forum is an excellent place for solving specific problems. With numerous active users, it's a community-driven resource where one can get answers to Excel queries quickly.

3. **Exceljet.net**
   - Known for its clean layout and straightforward guides, Exceljet offers quick tips, tricks, and shortcuts to enhance your Excel skills. The site's focus on practical usability makes it a favorite.

Professional Organizations and Groups

1. **International Association of Microsoft Certified Professionals (IAMCP)**
   - Joining professional groups such as IAMCP can provide networking opportunities with other Excel professionals and enthusiasts who are eager to share their knowledge and experience.

2. **Local Meetup Groups**
   - Platforms like Meetup often have groups dedicated to Excel and data analysis. These meetings can be invaluable for learning from experienced users and seeing how others solve real-world data problems.

Conferences and Workshops

1. **Microsoft Ignite**
   - Microsoft's annual conference features workshops and seminars that are specific to Excel and the broader Microsoft 365 suite. These are opportunities to learn from the developers of Excel and to network with other professionals.

2. **Data Visualization Summits**
   - These conferences focus on the art and science of data presentation, an essential skill for advanced Excel users who need to communicate data effectively.

In a field as dynamic as data analysis, continuous learning is key. The resources listed above provide avenues to keep your skills sharp and your knowledge current. Whether through books that delve into complex topics, online courses that offer interactive learning experiences, blogs that provide quick tips, or professional groups that facilitate networking, each resource offers unique benefits. By engaging with these resources, you ensure that your journey with Excel continues beyond the basics, steering towards a path of expert proficiency and insightful data manipulation.

GLOSSARY

Navigating the world of Excel involves a plethora of terms and jargon that can be intricate for beginners and even for those with intermediate knowledge. This glossary serves as your compass through the landscape of Excel terminology, ensuring that each concept not only becomes clear but also accessible. Here, we decode the language of Excel, providing succinct definitions that aim to enhance your understanding and operational skills within this powerful software.

Absolute Cell Reference

- **Definition**: A cell reference that remains constant even if the formula is copied or moved to another cell. Denoted by dollar signs, as in **$A$1**.

Absolute Reference

- **Definition**: A cell reference in a formula that remains constant, even if the formula is copied or moved to another cell. It is denoted by dollar signs ($), as in $A$1.

Active Cell

- **Definition**: The currently selected cell in a spreadsheet, where data entry or edits will be made. It is highlighted by a thicker border around the cell.

Array

- **Definition**: A collection of items stored at contiguous memory locations. In Excel, an array can be a single row or column of values, or a multi-dimensional matrix of data.

Array Formula

- **Definition**: A formula that performs multiple calculations on one or more items in an array. Array formulas can return either multiple results or a single result. They are entered by pressing Ctrl+Shift+Enter.

Binary Worksheet

- **Definition**: A sheet in a workbook saved in a binary file format (.xlsb), which can accommodate larger data sets and complex spreadsheets more efficiently than the standard format.

Cell Style

- **Definition**: Predefined formatting options that can be applied to cells to ensure consistency in formatting across a worksheet or workbook.

Conditional Formatting

- **Definition**: A feature that changes the appearance of cells based on specific conditions. This can include changing colors, applying formats, and adding icons based on the data's value.

Data Model

- **Definition**: An integrated view of the data linked from multiple tables, effectively building a relational data source inside an Excel workbook.

Data Validation

- **Definition**: A set of rules that dictate what data can be entered into a cell. This can help prevent data entry errors by restricting the types of data that can be inputted.

External Reference

- **Definition**: A reference to a cell or range on a sheet outside the current workbook. It is denoted by the workbook and worksheet name, like '[Budget.xlsx]Annual!C10'.

Excel Add-In

- **Definition**: A supplemental program that adds extra features to Excel, typically written in VBA or .NET frameworks.

Field

- **Definition**: A column in the dataset. In database terms, it represents a category of information, such as 'Last Name' or 'Sales Total'.

Filter

- **Definition**: A tool used to display only the rows in a spreadsheet that meet specified criteria, hiding the rows that do not match.

Financial Functions

- **Definition**: Functions that are used to perform financial calculations, such as rate of return, depreciation, and payments. Examples include **PMT**, **FV**, and **NPV**.

Formula Bar

- **Definition**: The bar at the top of the Excel window that displays the data or formula contained in the active cell. It is also where you can enter or edit data and formulas.

Function

- **Definition**: A predefined formula in Excel that simplifies complex calculations. Functions require specific parameters and can be used for mathematical, statistical, financial, and logical operations among others.

Gridlines

- **Definition**: The lines that separate cells on a worksheet. These can be formatted, shown, or hidden.

Input Range

- **Definition**: A range of cells that contain data used in calculations or analysis.

Header and Footer

- **Definition:** Areas at the top and bottom of a worksheet page that can contain data or images. Headers and footers are typically used to add titles, dates, or page numbers.

HLOOKUP Function

- **Definition**: Similar to VLOOKUP, but searches for a value in the first row of a table array and returns a value in the same column from a specified row.

Justify

- **Definition**: A formatting option that aligns text within a cell to both the left and right margins, adding space between words as necessary.

Logical Functions

- **Definition**: Functions that test for true or false conditions and make logical comparisons between values. Examples include **IF**, **AND**, and **OR**.

Lookup Functions

- **Definition**: Functions that search for specific values within a data set. Examples include **VLOOKUP**, **HLOOKUP**, and **MATCH**.

Macro

- **Definition**: A recorded sequence of instructions to automate repetitive tasks within Excel. Macros are written in Visual Basic for Applications (VBA) and can range from simple to highly complex scripts.

Merge Cells

- **Definition**: Combining two or more adjacent cells into a single cell. This is often used in formatting to center a title over a particular section of a spreadsheet.

Macro Recorder

- **Definition**: A tool within Excel that records user actions as a macro script, allowing repetitive tasks to be automated.

Merge and Center

- **Definition**: A feature that combines selected cells into a single cell and centers the content within the merged cell.

Named Range

- **Definition**: A descriptive name assigned to a cell or range of cells. Named ranges make formulas easier to understand and maintain as opposed to using cell addresses like A1 or R1C1.

PivotTable

- **Definition**: A powerful tool that summarizes large amounts of data quickly and easily. Tables can be rearranged dynamically to display different aspects of the data, and calculations can be inserted to summarize or analyze the data further.

Range
- **Definition**: A selection of two or more cells on a spreadsheet. Ranges can be contiguous (e.g., A1:A10) or non-contiguous (e.g., A1, A3, A5).

Relative Reference
- **Definition**: A cell reference that changes when the formula containing it is moved to another cell. For example, if a formula with the reference A1 is copied to B1, it adjusts to B1 automatically.

Spreadsheet
- **Definition**: A digital worksheet. It's a collection of cells arranged in rows and columns to organize, analyze, and store data. Each cell can contain numeric or text data, or the results of formulas that automatically calculate and display a value based on the contents of other cells.

Statistical Functions
- **Definition**: Functions used for statistical analysis, such as averages, medians, and standard deviations. Examples include **AVERAGE**, **MEDIAN**, and **STDEV**.

Volatile Functions
- **Definition**: Functions that cause the cell in which they reside to recalculate every time Excel recalculates. Examples include **RAND()** and **NOW()**.

VLOOKUP Function
- **Definition**: A function that searches for a value in the first column of a table array and returns a value in the same row from a specified column.

Workbook
- **Definition**: An Excel file containing one or more sheets. Workbooks help to organize related sets of data across multiple spreadsheets within a single file.

Workbook Protection
- **Definition**: Security feature that restricts users from making structural changes to a workbook, such as adding or deleting worksheets.

Worksheet

- **Definition**: A single sheet within a workbook. It's the primary place where data is stored, manipulated, and analyzed.

Worksheet Protection

- **Definition**: A security setting that prevents changes to the worksheet's content, format, or both, allowing you to control which parts of the spreadsheet can be modified.

This glossary is designed not just as a reference but as a learning tool to deepen your understanding of Excel. It bridges the gap between simple spreadsheet usage and more advanced data manipulation techniques, enabling you to fully leverage Excel's capabilities in your professional and personal data tasks. By familiarizing yourself with these terms, you prepare yourself to navigate Excel's complex features with greater confidence and clarity.

Scan this QR CODE to access EXTRA CONTENT VIDEO:

Top Excel Tips and Tricks 2024 in Just 10 Minutes

Scan this QR CODE TO ACCESS

20 Essential Exercises to Improve Your Excel Skills

Made in the USA
Coppell, TX
13 September 2024